CLIENT SELF-DETERMINATION IN SOCIAL WORK

A Fifty-Year History

FELIX P. BIESTEK, S.J., D.S.W

Loyola University, Chicago, Illinois

CLYDE C. GEHRIG, PH.D.

Alma College, Alma, Michigan

LOYOLA UNIVERSITY PRESS

Chicago, Illinois 60657

44805

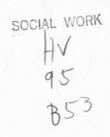
© 1978, Loyola University Press

Printed in the United States of America

LIBRARY OF CONGRESS
CATALOGING IN PUBLICATION DATA

Biestek, Felix Paul, 1912-
   Client self-determination in social work.

   Includes bibliographical references and index.
   1. Social service—United States—History.   2. Welfare
recipients—Attitudes.   I. Gehrig, Clyde C., 1935-   joint
author.   II. Title.

HV95.B53   361'.973   78-14225

ISBN 0-8294-0275-6 (cloth);   ISBN 0-8294-0276-4 (paper)

CONTENTS

INTRODUCTION

THE SOCIAL WORK PROFESSION is a complex mix of idealism and realism.

It selects as its supreme value the innate dignity and value of the human person. It maintains that nothing in the world is more precious and noble than the person, and that every person is worthy of respect. Social work, of course, is not alone in subscribing to this value. It is common to many other professions and to most cultures and societies. It is rooted in the Judaeo-Christian traditions and religions, and is enunciated in the bill of rights and constitution of many governments.

Social work, however, has chosen as its special concern a segment of the population whose dignity and worth are frequently in jeopardy. These people are variously named: the poor, the problem-laden, the economically unproductive, the

1

victims of unjust social structures, the disadvantaged, the abandoned, the underdog. They include the alcoholic on Skid Row, the child abuser, the violent patient in a mental hospital, the drug addict and pusher. Generally they are people who cannot pay for social services, people who have oppressive needs and problems that make them heavily dependent upon society's philanthropy. The social work profession, in its idealism, considers the social failures and the social successes as absolutely equal in terms of their fundamental human dignity and worth.

There are, of course, some social workers in private practice whose clients can and do pay fees, and some agencies such as child guidance and adult mental health clinics whose patients come from the middle and upper socioeconomic strata. But, historically and currently, the poor and the disadvantaged are the principal and numerically the largest group receiving social services.

The clientele that social work has chosen as its primary concern are people who are most likely to be the targets of rudeness, discourtesy, neglect, and disrespect. And that is why they were chosen: to prevent them from losing their sense of dignity and worth, to help them preserve self-respect in the midst of problems.

No other profession has such an exclusive concern for this group. There are schools, medical clinics, churches, and legal aid agencies in run-down neighborhoods, but education, medicine, religion and law have a more universal clientele. They do not "specialize" in the poor and needy as social work does.

The clients of social agencies are people with strengths and weaknesses, but their weaknesses are usually more visible. Our society would, if it could, deny their number or the depth of their problems, and if this failed, segregate and hide them. Some segments of society are inclined to attribute their problems to defects of character, laziness, or self-inflicted evils. They are considered victims of their own disorder rather than of ineffective and unjust structures of society.

The *realism* of the social work profession is exemplified by its commitment, in its helping methods, to perceive and deal with the client (be it individual, group, or community) as it is objectively. The objectivity includes the strengths and weaknesses of the client, his lovable and unlovable characteristics, his positive and negative feelings, his constructive and destructive attitudes and behaviors. Such realism is considered essential to the therapeutic goals; it is thought to be necessary for the effectiveness of the helping process. Idealization of the client, which is a denial of a segment of reality that is not favorable to the client, is considered unprofessional practice. It would be a refusal to accept and deal with the client as he really is. Social workers believe that idealization would vitiate the value and worth of the person.

If social work were to be placed on a scale measuring the level of abstraction of academic or professional disciplines, it would probably be at the lowest extreme of the spectrum. Philosophical metaphysics would probably be judged to be the most abstract, because it prescinds from all reality except first principles. Mathematics would probably be second; its exclusive interest is the measurement of quantities. Social work practice prescinds from nothing; it has no degree of abstraction. Every need or problem of an individual, group, or community is a potential concern—economic, emotional, medical, legal, or whatever. This does not mean that the social worker functions as a medical doctor, a lawyer, or a psychiatrist, but it does mean that he helps the client, by referral at least, to seek the necessary services. Certainly the emotional component of any human problem is a potential area for social service.

This combination of idealism and realism has critics—many and varied critics. Social work has been accused of being naive about people but cynical about social structures and institutions, believing that the latter have never been adequate enough to meet people's problems, and have always been unjust to the people at the lower socioeconomic levels. Social workers have been accused of stressing the rights of clients but not their obligations.

A more subtle and complex criticism is that the supreme value of social work is largely nullified by the manner in which the principle of client self-determination is practiced. On the one hand, social workers have been accused of interpreting client self-determination so liberally that it amounted to license, to unlimited freedom; while on the other hand, critics have claimed that self-determination in practice is nothing more than seductive manipulation, deceitful authoritativeness, over-all double dealing.

Client self-determination is the first logical consequence and test of the supreme value; usually it is accorded second place in the hierarchy of social work values. It declares that the human person has an innate right to make choices and decisions in those things that affect his life. To deprive him of that right is to deny his dignity and worth.

The right to freedom, to self-determination, is one of the most difficult of human values to comprehend. It contains so many variables that descriptions and definitions are precarious and hardly ever satisfying. Philosophers have struggled with it for ages and continue to do so today. It appears to be an ever-changing concept, affected by innumerable contemporaneous happenings in the culture in which it is found.

One would tend to hope that if the concept "human liberty" were studied in a circumscribed context, for instance, if it were limited to the field of social work, and specifically to the client as he receives help from a social agency—one would hope that the concept would be more easily defined and univocally understood. But, that does not seem to be the case. The meaning of the principle of client self-determination in social work, as will become apparent in this book, has been a controversial topic ever since the beginnings of professional social work in the United States.

Client self-determination is the focal point of the value system in social work. It is essential to the implementation of the supreme value; without self-determination, human dignity and worth are meaningless. Likewise, self-determination appears to be necessary if other values are to have meaning. Unfortunately, there is no listing of values that is generally accepted in the social work profession. The National Association of Social

Workers' *Code of Ethics* is the closest we have to an official index of values. There have been a number of attempts to catalogue them. The following are found in almost every list: individualization, self-determination, confidentiality, and right to self-realization. The only unanimity appears to be the human worth as the supreme value.

And so we approach the reason for this book. The principle of client self-determination, though not the supreme value, is the strategically most pervasive value. It is necessarily implied in all the values. Social work values are understood and applied insofar as self-determination is understood and applied.

The social work profession, therefore, must be perennially committed to studying this value. How study it? A theoretical approach is one option: attempting a clarification through conceptual analysis. A historical approach is another option and is the one employed here, because it appeared to be a better way to record an elusive, very complicated, living concept.

This book is a fifty-year history (1920 to 1970) of the concept, value, principle (call it what you will) of the client's right to free choice and decision concerning himself in the social work context. The story of each of the five decades begins with brief references to the political, economic, and social events which characterize the decade and which set the scene for the development of the theory and practice of the principle of client self-determination in that time period. The history is based upon the social work literature, principally of the United States. Care has been taken to identify the source of significant items of this history.

Beginnings_____ Influence of
socioeconomic conditions _____
_____Theory of client freedom_____
_____ Problems _____ Practice _____

CHAPTER 1

1920—1929

THIS WAS a decade of beginnings.

In the history of nations, as World War I was terminated by the Treaty of Versailles on June 28, 1919, a new Europe was created. The boundaries of a number of countries were altered and a few new nations were born.

In the United States, it was the decade of three Presidents: Harding (1920-1923), Coolidge (1923-1928), and Hoover (1928-1932). The population was 106,466,000 and growing rapidly; by 1970 it would almost double to 203,166,000. Labor unionism, after some forty years of underground struggling, was emerging into a socially respectable movement; in 1920 the American Federation of Labor counted five million members. Radio became a commercial enterprise; the first regular broadcasting station, KDKA in Pittsburgh, was established in 1920. Although

6

the airplane was already in use in the previous decade, the solo transatlantic flight of Charles Lindberg in 1927 contributed significantly to the growth and development of aviation.

A different type of beginning was Prohibition, the 18th Amendment to the United States Constitution and the Volstead Act, which prohibited the manufacture and sale of intoxicating liquors. It lasted from 1919 to 1933 and was the occasion for the rise of illegal alcoholic traffic and of gangland warfare. There was an economic depression from 1921 to 1926, a rather mild one as compared to the subsequent one. This was followed by a few years of unprecedented prosperity which ended abruptly with the stock market crash in October 1929, which gave birth to the Great Depression.

The effects of the huge immigration from 1901 to 1910 began to be fully felt in the early part of this decade. Almost nine million people, mostly unskilled and uneducated from Southern Europe, poured into the United States and settled in the larger cities. In 1924 the National Origins Quota Law was passed to control the influx.

Many beginnings in social work occurred at this time. The American Association of Medical Social Workers began in 1918, the American Association of School Social Workers in 1919, the American Association of Social Workers in 1919, and the American Association of Psychiatric Social Workers in 1926. The journal, *The Family* (later to become the *Journal of Social Casework*), published its first issue in 1920. *The Compass*, a bulletin of the National Social Workers' Exchange first appeared in 1920; in June of 1921 it became a publication of the A.A.S.W. The *Social Service Review* began publication in March 1927. In social work education, the Association of Training Schools for Professional Social Work was organized in 1929 (this was the predecessor of the American Association of Schools of Social Work and of the current Council on Social Work Education). In 1920, fifteen schools were members of this Association; in November of 1929, there were twenty-five schools, with an enrollment of 1,306. The first code of ethics for social workers was drafted in 1923 in an institute of the Charity Organization

Society sponsored by the Russell Sage Foundation. It appeared only in mimeographed form. An officially sanctioned code of ethics was not adopted by the profession until two decades later.

Two occurrences exerted an important influence upon social casework: Mary Richmond's book, *Social Diagnosis* (1917), and the debut of psychiatry into social work. Richmond's contribution was directed to making social casework, and specifically the social study process, more systematic and scientific. The assumption seemed to be that if the social worker really knew all of the pertinent facts, the problem of the client would be more accurately diagnosed, and hence the treatment would be more effective. Psychiatry, prior to World War I, had a poor public image and was attacked severely and widely. After the War, due to the work of psychiatrists with the mental health casualties of military personnel, its popular image improved considerably, and more pertinent to our interest here, it was discovered as a valuable source of knowledge by many social workers. It was considered by many caseworkers in this decade as a potential gold mine for all three functions: study, diagnosis, and treatment. The impact of psychiatry grew steadily throughout the following decades.

The socioeconomic conditions that most directly affected casework and the principle of client self-determination were (1) immigration, (2) the 1921-1926 economic depression, and (3) the public image of social work.

The presence of large numbers of immigrants in the general population and consequently in the case loads of social agencies caused problems.[1] The language and culture differences made casework more difficult because it was harder to establish the desirable relationship. The immigrant clients, disappointed in their expectations of their newly adopted country, frequently approached the social agencies with much reserve and even with distrust. Caseworkers were tempted to assume the attitude that these incommunicative clients had a greater need for instruction and direct guidance than for self-determination in regard to planning for their social and economic problems. Manipulation seemed so reasonable, in the circumstances, and so much more efficient. It frequently seemed to caseworkers a waste of time to explain, often with the aid of interpreters, the casework process. It seemed so much quicker for the caseworker to go ahead and do for the client what the caseworker thought best. Moreover, many of the clients came from countries where the democratic approach, especially in regard to the poorer classes, was unknown. In their native countries they were unaccustomed to being consulted for their opinions by representatives of public or private agencies of whatever sort.

The second socioeconomic condition which also tempted caseworkers to veer away from the principle of self-determination towards manipulation was the economic depression of 1921 and its subsequent effects.[2] The size of the case loads grew substantially. The caseworkers of necessity had to make the most efficient use of their time. In such circumstances client self-determination seemed like a luxury that agencies did not seem to be able to afford. Moreover, the clients, at least to external appearances, seemed to assess the receipt of material and financial assistance above refinements such as self-determination. They needed food, clothing, and shelter and were impatient with any delay, even that caused by the worker's attempts to give this service in accord with the democratic principle of casework.

The third condition which affected the theory and practice of the principle of self-determination, as seen in the casework literature, was the general public's lack of understanding of social work. As the titles of the references indicate,[3] during this period social workers displayed considerable concern about the methods of interpreting (the term "selling" was frequently used) social work to the general public. One of the obvious ways of interpreting was to "show results"; that could be easily seen and understood by everyone. Such results, caseworkers were again tempted to feel, would be more easily obtainable through the direct action of the caseworker via manipulation. The democratic approach towards the poor and unemployed seemed to be a fine point, to be sacrificed temporarily until the general public grew more favorable and more understanding.

Such, in broad strokes, was the environment in which the principle of client self-determination began and developed.

THEORY

In examining the casework literature of this decade, the first item of interest is the terminology which was used to designate the generic concept of client freedom. Five descriptive phrases were used:

1. Client participation

   The Milford Conference said: "Participation is a name used to designate the method of giving to a client the fullest possible share in the process of working out an understanding of his difficulty and a desirable plan for meeting it."[4]

2. Client responsibility for plan-making

   According to Mary Richmond: "Human beings are not dependent and domestic animals. This fact of man's difference from other animals establishes the need for his participation in making and carrying out plans for his welfare."[5]

3. Self-help

   Henry C. Schumacker wrote: "Emphasis must be placed on the desirability and necessity of self-help on the part of the individual and his family."[6]

4. Self-direction

   Frank J. Bruno, in discussing cooperation between the social worker and the client, said: "Each person is a center of social energy possessing the capacity of self-direction. . . ."[7]

5. Self-expression

   Karl De Schweinitz said: "Puzzled, bewildered, and buffeted though a man may be he never loses the urge to self-expression. No matter how submissive he may have become to another's suggestion, no matter how prone he may be to turn to some one else for the solution of his problems, when he reaches that which to him is vital he wants to be the arbiter of his own desires."[8]

The term "self-determination" was used by Winfred Rhoades and Frank J. Bruno, but only in reference to the nature of man and not specifically as a working principle of casework.[9]

The five phrases listed above were not regarded as technical terms; they were used interchangeably, sometimes by the same author, for essentially the same concept. The common denominator seemed to be that the client be given the fullest possible share in the process of developing an understanding of his difficulty and a desirable plan for meeting it.

No writer in this decade attempted to formulate a complete description or a formal definition of client freedom in casework. However, a number of scattered, fragmentary comments are found in the literature. These pieces, assembled and arranged, can form a statement of how the concept of client self-determination was understood at this time. The statement consists of seven propositions:

1. Caseworkers sometimes are tempted to impose a plan of their own making upon the client.[10]

2. The client, like every person, has a desire to govern his own life, to make his own decisions, to be the arbiter of his own desires, to share the responsibility in the casework process, and to feel a sense of ownership in the treatment plan. Even when he is puzzled and bewildered he does not want a plan superimposed on him, but wants to be a participant in the helping process, beginning with the first contact.[11]

3. His freedom is not to be violated even to help him. He can acquire social and economic responsibility and self-maintenance only from suffering the consequences of his own mistakes and learning by his own failures and successes.[12]

4. Effective casework treatment is possible only when the client voluntarily participates in the process, and when the caseworker respects the client's own views and solutions of his difficulty. Thus is brought into play every force that can aid the client's individual and social adjustment.[13]

5. In order to promote the client's participation, the objective of the caseworker is to help the client make his own decisions by

planning with him, by stimulating his thinking, and by supplying adequate motives.[14]

6. The specific function of the caseworker is to help the client see the facts of the situation, to suggest, advise, interpret, and guide, but in such a way that the decision will really be the client's own.[15]

7. The caseworker should avoid assuming responsibilities and making decisions that rightfully belong to the client.[16]

Thus was the concept of client freedom understood in this decade. It is the statement of an ideal to be striven for, however, rather than of the actual practice. As this chapter will show, the ideal had been qualified by reality considerations in some cases; every client was not equally capable of making decisions for himself. Moreover, many practical difficulties arose in applying the ideal to practice.

What importance was attributed to client freedom? Some writers considered it as an essential operative principle. Richmond called it "the policy of all others" and one of "the foundation stones" of the social work "philosophy."[17] De Schweinitz referred to it as being at the root of one's philosophy.[18] Cannon called it "a principle inherent in social work."[19] Mohr regarded it as one of "the fundamentals of casework."[20]

Others stressed its necessity for effectiveness in the helping process: the quality of service and treatment was in direct proportion to the free participation of the client in decision-making.[21]

A few stressed the conviction that individuals in a real democracy have a right and a need for self-planning.[22]

There was a beginning awareness in the literature of this decade that the basic right of human freedom is not unlimited; limitations are necessary in every type of social living. The casework client, likewise, cannot exercise an absolute and unlimited freedom in choosing and deciding. A few limiting factors were briefly discussed in the literature.

1. The capacity to act freely varies from client to client. It is the function of the caseworker to gauge the capacity of clients to assume responsibility for their own plans and decisions.

> Effective treatment likewise demands that the social caseworker shall be able to gauge the tempo and ability of the client in assuming responsibility.[23]

2. The client should be free only after there is evidence that he is governed by his intelligence rather than by his emotions.

> When the client gave evidence of . . . a change from emotional to intelligent behavior . . . she was left free to act for herself.[24]

3. The caseworker should not blindly endorse every idea or plan proposed by the client; it must be realistic.

> Although it is important to leave the individual free to make his own plans, this does not mean that one should blindly endorse every idea that is proposed by the person who comes for advice. The plan must be genuine and must have a reasonable chance of success. . . .[25]

It appears rather clear from the above quotations that the caseworker was considered the final arbiter concerning the limitations. She decided if the client were capable of responsible and intelligent decision-making and if the plan had a reasonable chance of success.

PROBLEMS

This gave rise to a few questions and difficulties. De Schweinitz asked what is to be done when the client, after considerable discussion, adamantly fixed upon an unsound plan. His answer was ". . . under the circumstances it may be wisest to help him to learn in the only way by which, after all, most people learn, that is by experience."[26]

He pursued this a bit further and inquired what was to be done if the unsound plan appeared to endanger his health or morals. His answer was:

To learn by experience is expensive, and when health and morals are at stake it would seem dangerous to assume the responsibility of making an unwise experiment possible.[27]

Purdy responded to the question similarly:

Whatever may be our faith concerning God and man, we can all accept as our ultimate goal the clearing away of all obstacles to the fullest development of body, mind, and soul for time and eternity.[28]

Everett replied differently:

The social worker . . . has to cast aside any preconceived ideas of the right and wrong of human conduct, to learn to take what she finds and to devote herself to understanding why it is so.[29]

It is not clear from Everett's statement whether she was advocating a value-free profession, or simply saying that values are not imposed on clients.

De Schweinitz asked another question: In the case of the client who sets his heart on an unsound plan, should force be used? His answer was that the use of any type of force was generally a confession of the failure of adequate knowledge and skill, and he illustrated his conviction.

A man who was ill with tuberculosis was unwilling to go to a sanatorium. Yet, his carelessness and his failure to take precautions were menacing the health of his children. A (private) social agency which had been supporting the family refused to continue to supply financial assistance so long as he remained at home. The man agreed to enter the sanatorium. After he had been there three months, he returned. When persuasion did not succeed in inducing him to go back, the refusal to support accomplished this purpose. Again he came home, and again the process was repeated. Altogether he was admitted three times to the sanatorium. Three times he returned, and doubtless, it was only his death at the sanatorium which prevented him from coming back once more. This shows the effectiveness and the ineffectiveness of force. The man went to the sanatorium, but he had nothing within himself to keep him there; yet, on the other hand, the use of force sent him back and saved his wife and children from contracting the disease.[30]

He raised another type of difficulty: what should be done when the client wants the caseworker to make the decisions for him, when the client is overly dependent and does not want to assume the responsibility for decisions? The answer was to "place responsibility upon him and to expect accomplishment of him," but the amount and degree of the responsibility placed upon the client should be carefully geared to his strength.

> There is nothing more difficult in the art of helping than this, for one must maintain a nice balance between doing everything and doing nothing, varying the weight of responsibility according to the strength of the individual who is being helped. This calls for the most intimate knowledge of the person in difficulty, and even then, one is frequently at a loss to know how much or how little achievement should be expected of him.[31]

Brisley posed a question concerning the advocacy role of the social workers. It is a question that was far ahead of its time, probably the first time in the history of social work that the advocacy concept was introduced. "Should clients be allowed to choose the agency, and the visitors whom they wish, as they choose their physician and attorney?"[32] Brisley did not answer the question explicitly but implied an affirmative response. This concern will reappear, with fuller elaboration, in a subsequent chapter of this study dealing with the decade of the sixties.

Steger raised a question that probably many caseworkers asked themselves in their day-to-day work: is not this democratic principle a painfully slow process? The response was that it definitely was time consuming and probably would be abandoned if the caseworker lacked a deep faith in the potentialities of the human person.[33]

There were other questions and difficulties that were implied rather than explicitly stated:

• Is it legitimate for the caseworker to convince a client to adopt a definite course of action?[34]

● In applying the principle of client self-determination to the care of the aged, who are inclined to make unrealistic plans and unreasonable demands, what limitations to client freedom are legitimate? Who decides these limitations?[35]

● May a caseworker seek information from sources other than the client without the client's permission? If the client does not give permission, when the caseworker thinks the information is necessary to draft a sound plan, must the client's decision be respected?[36]

● Must the contents and results of the caseworker's diagnosis be completely revealed to the client, so as to help him reach a decision? If the caseworker does not share the diagnosis with the client, is the client deprived of a certain degree of self-determination?[37]

● Is it in conformity with client self-determination for the caseworker to "plant" an idea in the mind of the client, so that it will "germinate" and develop?[38]

● May a caseworker teach and instruct clients?[39]

PRACTICE

How closely did practice approximate theory? How did the literature of this decade evaluate the implementation of the principle of client self-determination in actual practice? As could be expected, the practice was mixed. A few over-all criticisms appeared in the literature; the following are illustrative.

> May we not confess, in all honesty, that there is still much of manipulation in casework, activity that does not strike deep into the life of the individual? Do not too many of our case records . . . still recount in stereotyped form the jerky, wooden movements of marionettes pulled this way and that by controlling strings?[40]

> To conceive of coercion in this age of individualism is preposterous. Yet, must we not confess that most of us are guilty of

"bossing" now and then? We are all loud in our condemnation of dictatorial manner, of withholding a necessity until the wisdom of our decision is acknowledged. But . . . people are seized, and after whirling about are dropped in bewilderment, if not in actual fright . . . such treatment can be compared to a cyclone.[41]

It would be grossly unfair to project these strictures to all practitioners of this decade; manipulation of clients was not the order of the day, but it did exist. Many points of view and many methods of practice were extant at this time. Samples of every stage of the evolutionary process through which social work had passed can be found.[42] Three stances were discernible.

1. *Explicit endorsement of manipulation.* The following statement is contained in an article which proposed to identify the casework techniques. A group of caseworkers analyzed ten case records and found eighty–six different techniques applied. Some of them are: "simulated agreement . . . minimizing the seriousness of the interviewee's position . . . jollying . . . flattery . . . humor . . . ."

> If . . . we decide it is practical, is it ethical to manipulate the behavior of human beings by techniques so laboriously mastered and so adroitly used? On the basis of some successful processes . . . I am ready to answer in the affirmative.[43]

2. *Explicit commitment to client self-determination with implicit denial of it.* Faults in implementing the principle were implicit and unintentional, due principally to the profession's early stage of development. For example, clarity, system, and specificity in case planning were emphasized at the time. The following excerpt from an article that described an experience in supervision illustrates the point. The article suggested a method of recording, but implicit in this proposal was the complete responsibility of the caseworker, with little or no reference to the client's involvement. The recording plan is here presented in the same form as it appeared in the article.[44]

Case A

PROBLEM	CAUSAL FACTORS	TREATMENT
Mrs. A's poor health.	Inability to make ends meet. Not sensible in regard to resting and eating and working. Possibly a functional organic disorder.	Keep her in touch with doctor and dispensary; change her habits of eating, etc., if possible. Persuade her to have a physical examination and send her on vacation with Susie.
Inability of relations to help. Sister's lack of hospitality.	Business depression. Cut in R.R. pay.	Become acquainted with relatives, especially sister, and gain their cooperation.
Narrow horizon of interests.	Limited schooling; absorption in petty worries.	Secure a good "friendly visitor" who will encourage Mrs. A. to interest herself in nature, books, moving pictures of better kind and so on.
Danger of Susie becoming neurasthenic.	An only child much influenced by mother.	Plenty of normal, healthy companionship. Guide her vocational interests.

3. *Explicit acceptance of client self-determination with a gross denial of it.* The following "treatment letter" was written by a caseworker who concluded her letter to the client by saying "The choice lies with you alone. When you have made your decision I shall be glad to hear from you." This caseworker, it would appear from her words, would subscribe to the principle of client self-determination. Her manner of putting the prin-

ciple into practice, however, was, at a minimum, historically interesting.

It should be historically significant, likewise, that this letter appeared in the professional casework journal at a time when there was considerable discussion of the democratic participation of the client. Moreover, it should be meaningful that the letter was taken very seriously by other caseworkers, as will appear below. Today it might be considered a burlesque of casework.

Serving as a historical example, it can also confirm the statement already quoted that "the philosophy of participation is more easily understood than is the method of achieving it."[45]

The letter in social treatment plays a part as important, though not as frequent, as the personal interview. Too often, however, as social records show, letters are written hurriedly and with little apparent appreciation of the probable reaction of the recipient. We present herewith a letter written by a family visitor to the man of the family who had run away from his responsibilities. He had gone to a small town where there was no social agency and no chance of having an interview with him by proxy.

What do you think of this as a treatment letter? Would it bring him back? We should be glad to have criticisms, suggestions, and discussion on it.

My dear Mr. Smith:

You and your family have been much on my mind in the past few weeks, because I feel a crisis has been reached in your lives. I need not tell you how keenly disappointed we have all been in you, because I am sure you must know it, and must feel the same disappointment in yourself.

But now that the break has come, we are looking to you as the only one who can mend it. By we, I mean your family and your friends, and among the latter I want you to count the Family Welfare Association.

I have seen much of your family in the last three weeks, as you no doubt know. I have been permitted to read your letters. Mr. Smith, I want you to feel that I understand your viewpoint, and can sympathize sincerely with you in your position. But I cannot think that you have helped solve your problem by running away from it. "Moonshine" is something you cannot run away from in this country, it is to be had anywhere you go if you look for it.

The only way to solve such a problem is to face it squarely and to fight it out with yourself. You have been strongly tempted, I know, but are you not man enough to resist what you know so well can bring nothing but sorrow to you and others? It is not a fight to be won in a day or a week. It is a fight that will take many weeks. But do you not think it worth the effort?

You have a family, too, to consider; three lovely children and a wonderful little wife. I wonder if you half realize just how wonderful she is? During this past winter and spring she has stuck to you through thick and thin and especially these past few weeks has she stuck, as few women have the courage to do. Much of the time since you left, she has been too ill to walk, yet she has kept up and going for the sake of your children.

As you know, Mary disappeared the same day you did. I shall never forget the look on Mrs. Smith's face when I had to tell her. If ever a woman needed her husband, she needed you then, but you were gone. And now, as a last straw, the children have taken the measles and the family is under quarantine. Yesterday when I was in your home, Mrs. Smith was caring for three sick children and getting Helen ready for her outing—all this, without a wink of sleep the night before. The previous day she received word of her brother's death.

Until you sent the $8, your family was almost entirely dependent upon Mrs. Brown and the landlady for support. They have seen that the children did not go hungry. You know better than I how able they are to do this.

Mr. White has paid the rent, although you are aware of the fact that he was without work all winter and had to meet all the doctor bills and funeral expenses for your mother.

You expected Mrs. Green and the Family Welfare Association to look after your family and keep them from going hungry. Mr. Smith, we cannot. We are entrusted with public funds which are to be spent to the best advantage to assist people in leading normal family lives. We would be untrue to our trust if we should support the family of any man when he is well, and strong, and able to work, but won't. There is no reason why you cannot support your family decently and give your children the advantages they deserve. When we support them for you, we only make it easier for you to escape your responsibility and keep from proving yourself a man. We cannot do that and at the same time claim to be your friends.

Since A ⸺ County cannot assume the care of its nonresidents, and we cannot oppose their policy, we shall advise Mrs. Smith to return to B⸺ as soon as the children are well enough. We cannot advise her joining you in the West, at least not until you have proved conclusively that you will provide for her and the children as you should. For the eight years of your married life she has followed wherever your fancy led you. Now we feel it time for you to establish a home permanently and settle down to the responsibilities of a real husband and father. So far, you must admit you have been rather a failure at both.

As for yourself and your plans for the immediate future, you must decide. If, after very careful consideration, you feel you can do best both morally and financially by working in the harvest, then do so. If you think it better to return to A⸺, face your problem like a man, and make the fight, we stand ready to help as far as we can. We should be glad to secure for you the medical services here provided for people suffering from your trouble. But you must understand that if you return, it means you are to support your own family and much differently than in the past, and there is to be no more dishonesty and no more shirking. There is to be a real home and a real head. If you become a citizen of A⸺, you are to be an asset and not a liability to our community.

Mrs. Smith has stood the test nobly, but there is a point beyond which no one can go. She is now close to that point. She cannot go through another experience such as the past winter and this summer have been. I earnestly hope it will not be necessary for her even to try.

I have tried to state conditions exactly as they are, neither exaggerating nor minimizing them. I hope you will think these things over most carefully, and make up your mind, once and for all, which road you will follow: the one requiring some self-denial and hard work, which leads to a real home and true happiness, or the one which you have been following, which leads to just what I have pictured in this letter. The choice lies with you alone. When you have made your final decision I shall be glad to hear from you.

Yours very truly,[46]

This letter was discussed in the "Correspondence" column of *The Family* in its three subsequent issues, and a similar letter appeared in April of that year.[47] These discussions, however, centered about the virtues and shortcomings of letters as treatment methods, and little criticism was expressed about the contents of the letter quoted above and the attitude of the worker to the client.

In summary, this was a decade when social work took a few steps toward becoming a profession. Organizations were formed, periodicals were begun, schools of social work were accepted by universities, thought was given to a code of ethics, and beginnings were made in constructing a theory of social work. As in the history of some other professions, practice preceded theory, both enriching each other cyclically. The beginnings of social work theory were difficult; social workers were eminently practical people, deeply immersed in the details that are necessary to help people realistically. They felt more comfortable with the concrete than with the abstract. But, they accepted the fact that theory was necessary, and this chapter narrates the effort and the problems they encountered with one principle.

In concluding this first decade, it is interesting to note some of the issues that were posed, in seminal form, which would grow full-blown into vital concerns in the 1960s and 1970s. The question about "the right to fail" raised the issue of the relationship of client self-determination to other major values in social work. The concept of advocacy (although the term itself was not used) was briefly introduced. A subtle manipulation was seen to be inherent in the casework processes of study, diagnosis, and treatment. And concern about "showing results" was an early

manifestation of the profession's later concern about accountability and about the need for empirical research to prove social
work's effectiveness.

ENDNOTES FOR CHAPTER 1

1   Ida L. Hull, "The Immigrant as a Factor in Social Work," *The Family*,
    October 1925, p. 171; Bradley Buell, "Organizing the Community for
    Immigrant Education," *The Family*, October 1925, p. 175; Elsa Hirsch,
    "A Polish Background," *The Family*, October 1925, p. 181; J. Rodriquez
    Pastor, "The Puerto-Rican Immigrant," *The Family*, November 1925,
    p. 208; Marion Yingling, "Malka," *The Family*, June 1926, p. 105; Ruth
    S. Camblon, "Mexicans in Chicago," *The Family*, November 1926, p.
    207; Venturia Manuila, "Social Backgrounds of the Roumanian Immig-
    rant," *The Family*, December 1926, p. 251; Venturia Manuila, "The In-
    visible Environment of the Immigrant," *The Family*, October 1923, p.
    160.
2   Frances Perkins, "An Experiment in the Application of Case Work
    Methods to a New Problem," *The Family*, April 1921, p. 25; Perkins,
    "Case Work with Unemployed," *The Family*, March 1921, p. 19; Helen
    K. Kempton, "Is Social Work Necessarily a Dangerous Occupation?,"
    The Family, April 1926, p. 53; Editorial, *The Family*, January 1922, p.
    210; Mamie Cohen, "The Report of an Employment Agency," *The Fam-
    ily*, November 1927, p. 220; Malcolm S. Nichols, "New Emphases in
    Family Social Work," *The Family*, October 1928, p. 188; Editorial, *The
    Family*, November 1927, p. 224.
3   Dorothy E. Wysor, "How Can We Interpret Social Work to the Public?,"
    The Family, December 1926, p. 248; Mary S. Routzahn, "The Use of Case
    Stories in Newspaper Publicity," *The Family*, October 1925, p. 168; John
    R. Brown, "Publicity Versus Propaganda in Family Work," *The Family*,
    May 1926; Mary and Evart Routzahn, "The Publicity Program," *The
    Family*, March 1928, p. 3; Ellen F. Wilcox, "The Measurement of
    Achievement in Family Case Work," *The Family*, April 1927, p. 46; Jean
    Proutt, "Publicity—Before and After," *The Family*, February 1930,
    p. 301.
4   Milford Conference, *Social Case Work, Generic and Specific* (New York:
    American Association of Social Workers, 1929), p. 24; Mary A. Cannon,
    "Underlying Principles and Common Practices in Social Work," *The
    Family*, July 1928, p. 166; Jean M. Lucas, "The Interview of Persuasion,"
    The Family, July 1924, p. 128; Mary E. Richmond, *What is Social Work*
    (New York: Russell Sage Foundation, 1922), p.258; Nichols, "Family So-
    cial Work," p. 190; Irma Mohr, "Training Apprentice Workers in Rural

Agency," *The Family*, February 1930, p. 300; George L. Warren, "Some Aspects of International Case Work," *The Family*, October 1930, p. 200.

5 Richmond, *What is Social Work*, p. 258; Lucille Corbett, "Plan and Treatment," *The Family*, March 1923, pp. 8-10; Anna Vlachos, "Opening The Way," *The Family*, October 1924, p. 153; Lucia B. Clow, "The Art of Helping: Through the Interview," *The Family*, July 1925, p. 131; Karl De Schweinitz, *The Art of Helping People Out of Trouble* (Boston and New York: Houghton Mifflin Co., 1924), p. 148.

6 Henry C. Schumacker, "Personality and Its Development As It Is Affected by Financial Dependency and Relief–Giving," *The Family*, July 1928, p. 142.

7 Frank J. Bruno, "Cooperation in Social Work," *The Family*, November 1929, p. 201; Richmond, *What is Social Work*, p. 174.

8 De Schweinitz, *Helping People Out of Trouble*, p. 140.

9 Winfred Rhoades, "Personalities—or Things," *The Family*, December 1922, p. 206; Bruno, "Cooperation in Social Work," p.201.

10 De Schweinitz; *Helping People Out of Trouble*, p. 139; Richmond, *What is Social Work*, pp. 139-40.

11 De Schweinitz, *Helping People Out of Trouble*, pp. 139-40; Richmond, *What is Social Work*, p. 110; Corbett, "Plan and Treatment," pp. 8-10; Milford Conference, *Social Case Work*, p. 30.

12 Lawson Purdy, "Goals in Social Work," *The Family*, October 1925, pp. 186-87; Frances Taussing, "A German Interpretation of Case Work In America," *The Family*, June 1928, p. 126; Schumacker, "Personality and Its Development," p. 141; Milford Conference, *Social Case Work*, p. 29.

13 E. G. Steger, "Standards in Social Case Work," *The Family*, January 1925, p. 235; Nichols, "Family Social Work," p. 29; Richmond, *What is Social Work*, pp. 171-73.

14 Clow, "The Art of Helping," pp. 8-10; Corbett, "Plan and Treatment," pp. 8-10; De Schweinitz, *Helping People Out of Trouble*, p. 155; George L. Warren, "Some Aspects of International Case Work," *The Family*, October 1930, p. 200; Mary S. Brisley, "An Attempt to Articulate Processes," *The Family*, October 1924, p. 159.

15 De Schweinitz, *Helping People Out of Trouble*, p. 155; Vlachos, "Opening the Way," pp. 153-57; Margaret Wead, "Sponsoring Immigrant Marriages as a Case Work Problem," *The Family*, April 1922, p. 30.

16 De Schweinitz, *Helping People Out of Trouble*, p. 168; Vlachos, "Opening the Way," p. 153.

17 Richmond, *What is Social Work*, pp. 109, 257.

18 De Schweinitz, *Helping People Out of Trouble*, p. 139.

19 Mary A. Cannon, "Underlying Principles and Common Practices in Social Work," *The Family*, July 1928, pp. 125-26.

20 Mohr, "Training Apprentice Workers," p. 300.

21 Richmond, *What is Social Work*, p. 258; Rhoades, "Personalities—or Things," p. 206.
22 Richmond, *What is Social Work*, p. 173; Corbett, "Plan and Treatment," pp. 8-10.
23 Milford Conference, *Social Case Work*, p. 29.
24 Vlachos, "Opening the Way," pp. 153-57.
25 De Schweinitz, *Helping People Out of Trouble*, p. 149.
26 Ibid., p. 149.
27 Ibid., p. 150.
28 Purdy, "Goals in Social Work," pp. 186-87.
29 Edith M. Everett, "Teaching Teachers," *The Family*, May 1926, pp. 71-73.
30 De Schweinitz, *Helping People Out of Trouble*, pp. 150-151.
31 Ibid., pp. 159-61.
32 Brisley, "An Attempt to Articulate Processes," p. 159.
33 Stager, "Standards in Social Case Work," pp. 223-24.
34 Helen L. Myrick, "Cross Examination and Case Work Interviewing: An Art," *The Family*, June 1926, p. 124.
35 Elizabetth Dutcher, "Care of the Aged from the Point of View of the Private Society," *The Family*, July 1926, p. 148.
36 M. J. Karpf, "Sociologists and the Social Worker Meet," *The Family*, April 1928, p. 44.
37 Ibid.
38 Janice M. Grant, "Treatment of Alcoholics," *The Family*, July 1929, p. 139.
39 Ibid.
40 Lucille Corbett, "Spiritual Factors in Case Work," *The Family*, December 1925, pp. 223-24.
41 Jean M. Lucas, "The Interview of Persuasion," *The Family*, July 1927, p. 157.
42 Jessie Taft, "The Spirit of Social Work," *The Family*, June 1928, p. 103.
43 Pearl Salsberry, "Techniques in Case Work," *The Family*, July 1927, p. 157; Joanna C. Colcord, "The Need of Adequate Case Work with the Unmarried Mother," *The Family*, November 1923, p. 170; Elizabeth Dutcher, "Principles Underlying Modern Casework with Relatives," *The Family*, July 1924, pp. 116-17.
44 Elizabeth L. Holbrook, "An Experiment in Supervision," *The Family*, October 1924, pp. 147-49.
45 Taft, "The Spirit of Social Work," p. 103.
46 Mary Jones, "Treatment by Letter," *The Family*, January 1925, p. 236-37.
47 Ann Smith, "Another Treatment Letter," *The Family*, April 1925, pp. 54-55.

CHAPTER 2

1930—1939

THIS was the decade of the Great Depression and of extensive social welfare provisions.

Following the stock market crash in 1929, more than 1500 banks closed, industry was crippled, many businesses failed, and almost 25 percent of the labor force was unemployed. The depression lasted from 1930 to 1936; it was the greatest economic calamity in American history.

President Franklin D. Roosevelt was elected in 1932 and immediately instituted the "New Deal," which included many relief provisions. The Civilian Conservation Corps, created on March 31, 1933 took a quarter of a million young men from poor families and employed them in soil conservation and reforestation projects. The Federal Emergency Relief Administration,

26

under the direction of Harry Hopkins, a social worker, was established in May 1933. Its purpose was to give federal aid to the states in dealing with relief. The Civil Works Administration, created in June 1933, provided employment for four million people to build and repair schools, highways, sewer systems, and airports. Aid was provided to the business sector via the National Recovery Administration (1933) and to farmers through the Agricltural Adjustment Act (1933). Organized labor was helped in 1934 by Section 7A of the National Industry Recovery Act and in 1937 by the Wagner Act. These Acts guaranteed the right to organize unions and bargain collectively.

The Social Security Act of 1935 was certainly the most important welfare program in American history, the broadest and most complicated legislation ever passed by Congress. It was administered by the federal government but many provisions were made for sharing and cooperating with the states. It included old-age pensions, unemployment compensation, aid to the blind, to other physically handicapped, and to dependent children. It was a controversial act. Many feared it as an entrance into socialism, but the depth and extent of impoverishment due to the depression made the Act, even in the opinion of most of its opponents, necessary and inevitable.

The depression, as could be anticipated, had a notable influence on the practice of social work and on the principle of client self-determination. Social workers were confronted with enormous economic needs for which the resources, in spite of the federal welfare programs enumerated above, were grossly inadequate. They had to shoulder huge case loads which caused overwork, harassment, and which sometimes undermined the social worker's health. In the midst of this turmoil, the caseworkers found that the concepts of client participation and self-determination, which up to this time were considered by some caseworkers as an ideal which was practical only in private agencies giving counseling service, was a means of lightening their own burden and actually providing more effective and efficient casework service.[1] Because of the pressure of work and in order to conserve both time and energy "A business-like approach to the client was adopted and there was a tendency to give the client more responsibility for making and executing his plans."[2]

This new emphasis upon client participation, originally initiated as a practical expedient, led to new insights. Those caseworkers who encouraged clients to assume more responsibility became enthusiastic about this procedure and felt that they had discovered new skills and new ways of accomplishing what they had thought was impossible.[3]

The effect upon clients was also noticeable; the responsibility with which they were entrusted contributed to self-esteem,[4] and they manifestly appreciated the active role in dealing with their problems.[5]

Another factor in the socioeconomic conditions which favorably affected the principle of self-determination was the coming of a new type of client to the social agencies. The twenty years since World War I had seen "the extension of social casework to large numbers of people who had never before had occasion to come into contact with it."[6]

First were the clients who came for psychiatric and counseling service, mostly child guidance clinics. The treatment of the emotional and relationship problems of children and parents, social workers knew, was incompatible with a dogmatic and authoritative attitude to clients. Child problems and complex family relationship problems could be alleviated only by the total involvement of clients in solutions which are their very own. And this conviction spread to other social services which strove for quality.[7]

> I suppose it is not strange that knowing clients as individuals and in relation to the more intimate aspects of their life should bring increasing respect for them as persons . . . and a wish to see them use to the utmost, and increase if possible, their powers of self-determination. This trend has not been peculiar to psychiatric social work but has permeated to some degree the practice of high-grade social casework everywhere.[8]

Second were the clients who came for financial assistance, but who belonged to the same social and economic class as the social workers. The depression made them dependent upon a social agency for the first time in their lives. Up to this time they were self-reliant and manifested a good capacity for adjustment. With such clients the social worker established more easily and quickly a client-partner relationship.[9]

THEORY AND PRACTICE

As in the previous decade, there was a variety of expressions for the concept of the client's freedom in the casework situation. The "participation" of the client, the most common term of the preceding decade, continued to be used,[10] but there was a noticeable disavowal of this word because it "implies subtle patronage of knowing what is right for the client and permitting him to help in the worker's plan."[11]

The absorption in the concept of "relationship" in these years caused a rebellion among caseworkers against the idea that it was the responsibility of the caseworker to create a plan and merely elicit the participation of the client; the dominant role shifted from the caseworker to the client. The right to plan for the client was recognized as belonging principally to the client. The words "self-help" and "making his own plans and decisions,"[12] practically used as synonyms, grew into more frequent use. Finally, the term "principle of self-determination" appeared, but almost exclusively in the writings of Bertha C. Reynolds.[13]

The importance of the principle was taken for granted. Seemingly almost everyone professed it, when stated in general terms, but differences and problems appeared as the principle was applied to different situations and settings. The most common reason proposed for its importance came from the increasing influence of psychiatry, namely, that self-determination was an essential condition of growth toward maturity.[14]

One of the most significant developments of this period was the new and vigorous interest in the concept of "relationship." It merits mention here because the autonomy of the client was posited as an essential ingredient of the client-worker relationship. It began with the publication of Virginia P. Robinson's book, *A Changing Psychology in Social Case Work*. The psychological base of her contribution was primarily Rankian, the orientation of the functional approach to casework as proposed by the Pennsylvania School. The book and the discussions that followed it made a deep and indelible impression.

> Early in 1931, a book became available to social workers which, it is safe to say, has created more discussion backed by strong personal feeling than anything in our short history as a profession. More, it has created searchings of heart and practice, questioning of old attitudes, tentative or whole-hearted experimentation, confusion, disappointment, hope of a more valid casework philosophy, despair of anything of the kind, a refuge for the passive, joy of power for the active—in short, the positive and negative effects of a most dynamic expression of living experience. . . .[15]

The relationship was elevated from an ancillary role, a mere bridge between the worker and the client over which pass the processes of study, diagnosis, and treatment, to a position of being treatment itself.[16] The reason for assigning this new importance to the relationship arose from the application of psychiatric concepts to social casework treatment.

> Psychoanalytic studies have now begun to show that the dynamic of change, in either attitude or behavior, lies in a relationship to a person. Since attitudes favor or stand in the way of the solution of many problems of social adjustment, the relationship between the caseworker and the client becomes a matter of extraordinary importance.[17]

Miss Robinson denounced the practice wherein the worker decided what was right for the client and then "motivated" him to accept and participate in the plan devised. She proposed a different approach:

. . . we see an increasing respect for the other individual accompanied by a corresponding reservation in taking active part in his affairs . . . technique lies rather in creating a relationship environment in which the individual growing process of the client can be released. This internal process itself then becomes the center, the growing point of change rather than any external manipulation of the client. . . .[18]

The impact of the new insights on the casework relationship was widespread, but it was misunderstood and misused by some, especially by social workers of the Diagnostic orientation who never bothered to learn about the fuller context of the relationship in the Functional orientation, the framework of Robinson's book. There were mild warnings that little knowledge about the "latest thing" was dangerous.[19] Gordon Hamilton's observation of what was happening was more critical: ". . . some case workers retreated into an almost mystical use of the worker-client relationship. We are just recovering from what one of my friends calls 'a silly season'."[20]

How did the caseworkers of this decade understand the principle of client self-determination? No one tried to define it; many referred to it. When the scattered references of many writers are pieced together, the following statements result:

1. The problem is the client's responsibility and remains so throughout the casework helping process.[21]

2. He has a right to decide whether he wants treatment and how much of it.[22]

3. The purpose of casework, then, is not to make changes in the client's life, but to give the client something for his own development which he was not able to extract from life by himself, something which will increase his capacity to make satisfactory adjustments in his life.[23]

> The newer method has much to commend it. It emphasizes the value of silence on the part of the worker; of listening to what the other wishes to talk about, rather than probing for what we wish to know; not of trying to change the attitude of the other person, but of helping him to change his own attitude; not of planning for, or even with him, but rather of encouraging him to make his own plans.[24]

Additional specificity was added as the role of the caseworker was discussed. First are statements of the negative—what social workers should not do:

1. Persuade.[25]
2. Directly change attitudes and behaviors; to manipulate.[26]
3. Do things for or to the client.[27]
4. Control and direct.[28]
5. Advise; to offer plans unsolicited.[29]
6. Assume responsibility for the case.[30]
7. Predetermine the conclusion.[31]
8. Give approval or disapproval.[32]

Second are the positive statements—what the function of the caseworker should be:

1. To be psychologically active in order to understand the client and outwardly passive to help the client act freely. The activity of the caseworker may consist of using intuition and theoretical knowledge, observing and evaluating words, actions, and emotions of the client, identifying with him, enriching his resources, and thus stimulatng the client to his own activity.[33]

2. To introduce stimuli which will activate the client's own resources. Specific stimuli are support, mobilization of external resources, release from fears and tensions, educational process, and interacting of personalities of worker and client.[34]

3. To create an environment in which the client can grow and work out his own problems.[35]

4. To give perspective to the client's problem.[36]

5. To help the client maintain his habitual patterns of living through self-directed use of funds.[37]

6. To offer suggestions without pressure.[38]

7. To help the client move along on his own problem, at his own pace.[39]

8. To combine a listening, receptive attitude with active participation.[40]

The above statements indicate some noticeable progress from the preceding decade. Caseworkers moved away from merely eliciting the participation of the client to recognizing his psychological need for self-direction and for sustaining his responsibility in decision-making. This, at least, was the theory of the time, and many caseworkers practiced it. The tone of much of the literature, however, was exhortatory; that is, this understanding of client freedom was being recommended to the many social workers who still operated in the ways of an earlier period.

There was an awareness in the casework literature of this decade that the ideal of every client being fully self-determined was unreal; that self-determination cannot be absolute and unlimited. Certain modifications in applying the principle must be made due to (1) the client's capacity; (2) authority; and (3) community standards.

1. *The Client's Capacity.* All clients do not have the same ability to make decisions and the same strengths to take responsibility for their own affairs. It is a part of the worker's professional function, therefore, to evaluate the capacity of the client for self-determination. Some clients can keep the full responsibility for the solution of their own problems, but others may be so impaired in their capacity for adjustment that they need to be treated as socially sick persons. The worker must be aware of the mental, physical, and emotional capacity of each client to act for himself, and give assistance accordingly.[41]

To expect initiative from some individuals is comparable to an attempt "to draw water from a well gone dry." There are people who must receive before they can give, who must be steadied before they can step forward. Some clients are almost physically unable to determine themselves and must not be forced to a greater degree of self-determination than they really have the capacity for.[42]

With certain clients it is necessary for the worker to assume a great deal more responsibility in the making of plans and carrying them out than with others. This calls for wisdom, skill, and courage on the part of the worker.[43] Fear of such service only reflects the insecurity of the worker, because service is an indispensable tool in casework. It is one of the means by which the worker meets the reality situation. There are people threatened by physical and mental ill health who do not see a problem or who fail to recognize its nature, and in such cases the worker's responsibility to the community demands that he be more active.[44]

In a few extreme instances, in emergencies, the worker may have to act as quickly as an ambulance surgeon, expecially in the case of the very ill or ignorant or inarticulate, but these instances will be rare, and will be recognized by that worker who generally follows the principle of client self-determination.[45]

2. Authority. The second factor which may call for modifications in applying the principle of client self-determination is authority. Just how the principle of client self-determination, which advocates the freedom of the client, is compatible with the various types of authority in society had been a problem in some settings.

> Social workers as a group and as individuals fear—as the Puritan feared witchcraft—the use of the work "authoritative" in speaking of their own approach or technic. Possibly our fear has developed as a reaction to the authority, used in the "good old days," of ordering and prescribing cures for all social ills, and its misuse in our present practices.[46]

The following is a summary of the convictions expressed about this possible conflict and about the elements that need to be clarified and harmonized.

a. A distinction must be made between an authoritative attitude and an authoritative approach. An authoritative attitude is a rigid, emotional, domineering manner, wherein the person of the caseworker is the only basis for the authority. An authoritative approach is the use of a legitimate, objectively existing civil ordinance or law.

An authoritative attitude in a caseworker is inadmissible, but the authoritative approach is sometimes necessary; it can be useful, but must be delicately and skillfully used.

> To me the authoritative approach is useful—but delicate and dangerous. It is fraught with catastrophe when accompanied by an authoritative attitude. We should master the art of applying the

authoritative approach in given situations in the public assistance field, in the court, and in private agencies.[47]

b. Authority is one of the important realities of organized society; it is an external control to which individuals must become adjusted, and it can be constructive.

We know if we are in touch with reality, that external controls do exist all around us. Some, like birth and death, are immutable. Others are born out of the social process and are constantly changing and variable. They are not determined by a just and impersonal force but by other human beings subject to human weakness. Even as we adjust to them, we have a right to change them through the proper channels but, for good or bad, nature and the will of the group must be taken into account.[48]

c. Authority is necessary in society, and rules and regulations must be employed by caseworkers in certain aspects of the public assistance programs, in corrective agencies, and sometimes in private agencies. The use of coercive force to compel submission to authority, however, should be avoided by caseworkers and relegated to other public servants.[49]

d. Ordinarily people accept authority and feel a need for it if it is fair, necessary, and purposeful. Hostility to authority is caused by the manner in which it is exercised or by other provocative factors. Some people, however, such as the socially or mentally ill, may have a neurotic or psychotic aversion to it.

Clients who come to a family agency represent a cross section of the total population in their reactions to authority. There are the normal people who make an adjustment without too great rebellion. They are in touch with reality and have learned to control their own wishes in relation to those of others . . . . There is a second group whose members range all the way from those with neurotic patterns to the definitely neurotic and psychotically ill. Another group, the delinquents and criminals who make up the case loads of agencies attached to the law, are seen only occasionally in the family agency. These last two groups have faulty development in relation to reality and to their feelings about people. The criminal and delinquent do not abide by the wishes of others but feel deep antagonism to society. . . . They must be the ones to dominate and control; hence their great difficulties with authority . . . . Caseworkers need to know something about this feeling of the client toward authority in order to know whether he will regard any demands on him as unfair.[50]

e. How authority is used is the prime consideration. The spirit, the manner, and the attitude of the caseworker are all-important. Moreover, the use of authority should be individuated and related to the capacity of the client and to the realities of a given situation. Finally, authority should be employed only after all other casework approaches have failed.[51]

The caseworker's function is to help the client, by means of the casework approach, to accept and adjust to the limitations to his freedom established by authority. The caseworker must not be defensive about authority but consider it an item in the reality situation. The final decision to accept or reject authority remains with the client who will be responsible for the favorable or unfavorable consequences of his decision.

There are limiting conditions for the practice of any profession, necessities which the practitioner must explain to the person as binding upon them both. . . . She says, "We shall have to do so and so. Is there any way that I can help you to adjust to this necessity?"[52]

In cases where the central problem discussed by the client is conflict between two paths of action—one involving anti-social behavior or a non-conventional act—the worker may be tempted to threaten and forbid it. Experience and psychology have taught us the futility of either. What is the worker's role? Again recognizing that the choice is the client's, the worker can sometimes help him postpone action, weigh the consequences, and have conscious control over his final decision. In the heat of the moment a client may threaten to steal. Without moralizing, the worker may grant that that is something he can do, but point out that there are consequences of arrest for stealing. The client might stop and think. He might restrain himself. . . . Many times this kind of discussion will not help, will not even be heard. But nothing else can be of help.[53]

It should be noticed in the above discussion that there was almost no reference to challenging or changing social institutions which were unfairly or unjustly exercising authority. The environment, which included legal authority, was considered a reality, to which the caseworker helped the client to adjust. The espousal of social action to modify unjust structures would not come until the decade of the 60s.

3. *Community Standards.* The third potential factor which might limit client freedom is the area of community standards. Community standards were distinguished from civil laws and ordinances. The former were described as the unwritten expected behaviors which were neither established nor sanctioned by law. Beyond this distinction, the meaning of "community standards" was very vague. No effort was made to say what the standards were, how they were established, by whom, and how they are known. Neither is "community" specified; does it mean the neighborhood only or is it extended to include the city, the state, and the nation?

What the literature seemed to be saying was that the community (however it be understood) was the provider of social services, and therefore the people who benefit from these services were in some ways accountable to the community. Just how they were accountable was not clear.

A corollary was that the social worker had a dual responsibility: to the client and to the community. In effect this meant that the social worker, in promoting the welfare of his clients, was obligated to remain within the standards of the community.

To confuse the issue, the mores and customs of ethnic, racial, and religious groups seemed to be included in "community standards." The reasoning was that these constitute realities in the environment of the client and that adjustment to these realities was desirable for healthy social functioning. If a client was contemplating to transgress the precepts of his subculture, he should be helped to reconsider, to weigh the consequences, and hopefully choose to conform. The basis for this reasoning, then, was not one of quasi-ethnical obligation to the community, but rather a therapeutic one—adjustment to social realities.

The possibility that the subcultures might be contrary on some points to established law or to the mainstream culture of the community was not considered. It was simply assumed that they were consonant.

Here is a summary of the principal convictions expressed in the literature on these issues:

a. The community has a stake in the social welfare of the individual, and social service is very much a community matter. This appears most clearly, but not exclusively, in public welfare.[54]

b. The community's interest and responsibility in social work is emphasized by the fact that the community, ultimately, is the financial support of social services.[55]

c. A minority among caseworkers insist that the needy person is the exclusive client in casework, that the community is not the client, that the caseworker is in no way an agent of the community, and that the caseworker has no obligation to help the client adjust to the standards of the community.[56]

d. The majority of caseworkers maintain that the client and the caseworker must observe the limitations and requirements of community standards, that the goal of treatment is neither rampant individualism nor undesirable conformity, but rather an individual adaptation on the part of the client which helps him into a sounder, more realistic social adjustment.[57]

e. Clients differ in their attitude to the limitations and demands springing from community standards.[58]

f. One of the functions of the caseworker is to help the client in his adjustment to the limitations created by community standards; client self-determination must operate with these limitations.[59]

g. In helping the client adjust to community standards, it is important that the caseworker make every effort to understand the client's conduct, rather than to communicate tolerance or intolerance of it. The person can and must be accepted without necessarily accepting his undesirable behavior.[60]

QUESTIONS AND PROBLEMS

In exploring the casework literature of this decade for explicitly raised questions and problems concerning the application of the principle to practice, the following were found. Some were general questions referring to casework in all settings while others referred to specific settings: medical, public welfare, corrections, and casework with adolescents. Bertha Reynolds raised the first few questions.

Question: Do clients want self-determination?

> Do clients want self-determination, however? Perhaps this is only another instance, like those of other remedies such as removal of tonsils or the provision of Americanization classes, in which social workers decide what clients should want and proceed to give to them . . . . Self-determination is thought by the social case-worker to be an essential condition toward maturity of personality but it may not be desired by the client either in itself or as a step toward a goal for which he has no conscious wish. . . .[61]

Answer: Clients are ambivalent about self-determination, on the one hand they desire the protection and security that comes from putting the responsibility for their decisions on someone else; on the other hand, they desire to be individuals, to make decisions, and to keep responsibility themselves. The function of the caseworker is to help the client work out a realistic balance between these two urges.

> As long as life lasts, human beings are forced to find some balance between the desire for protection, security, freedom from struggle, and the desire to be individual, to have new experience, control conditions, make decisions, and take responsibility.[62]

Question: Is client self-determination a beautiful theory but applicable only to exceptional clients or especially favored agencies?

> There is a considerable number of social case workers who would say without hesitation that self-determination for the client is a

beautiful theory but it applies only to exceptional clients or especially favored agencies. They point to those who believe in it as
idealists, who have never seen the realities of case work, who accept, so they say, only clients of considerable intelligence and
then refuse to deal with any but relatively unimportant and intan-
gible problems. Psychiatric agencies, in the minds of these
critics, usually fall into that category. If their clients have "real
problems," such as a need for relief, they are referred to agencies
which work on a more practical basis.[63]

Answer: Research is needed to determine whether and to
what degree client self-determination is realistically practicable
in various casework agencies and with various types of clients.

Never has a professional field been in greater need of painstaking
research. Perhaps each philosophy of casework has certain types
of clients or sets of conditions to which it is applicable. If that is so,
there is need of determining what those conditions are and how to
distinguish the clients.[64]

Question: What is the worker's role when the client is inclined
to a path of action which involves anti-social or non-
conventional behavior?
Answer: Rather than threatening, forbidding, or moralizing,
the caseworker can help the client stop and think, postpone
action, develop conscious control, prevent impulsive action,
and weigh the consequence of the act.[65]
Question: May the caseworker express disapproval of some
action characteristic of the client?
Answer: The caseworker may express disapproval provided:
(1) it is a natural and inevitable thing to do; and (2) it implies
approval of deeper values and of the fine qualities of the client.

Paradoxical as it may seem the very disapproval implies approval
of the deeper values which the family has been able to build up. It
is because there is something fine and worth holding to that the
worker can definitely censure the behavior which is threatening
Mr. S's own personal integrity, as well as his relationship to and
satisfaction in his home and family.[66]

Question: The plan of treatment in medical settings is determined by the medical authority; the caseworker's function is to help the patient accept and cooperate in the medical plan. Is this type of casework violating the patient's right to self-determination, or is it a realistic individualization of the principle?[67]

Answer: Public opinion sanctions the invasion of private rights in health matters by duly authorized medical services, and medical social workers frequently participate in this authority. The medical caseworker, therefore, may have to assume a more than ordinary responsibility, because client self-determination in certain serious matters of health might be too costly to the patient or to the community. This is an instance where the principle of self-determination may have to be reduced to a minimum.

> The field of medical social work presents a problem to those who are confused by failure to make these discriminations. An exponent of the new philosophy shocks a medical social worker by failing to follow a case in which neglect of a child's eyes may result in blindness—this, because the family has not indicated any desire for service. The medical case worker takes responsibility for prevention when the education of the parents in self-determination would be at too great a cost to the child.[68]

Question: To what extent can incurrable cancer patients determine whether they should remain at home or be placed in an institution?

Answer: The patient's wishes must sincerely be respected but they must also be balanced by various factors in the reality situation. It is the function of the caseworker to effect this balance and then to help the patient accept a final plan. The factors may include the availability of institutional care, the patient's attitudes to home care and to institutional care, and the effect of home care upon the other members of the home.[69]

Question: How does the principle of self-determination apply to casework with patients who are afflicted with a communicable disease such as syphilis?

Answer: Social caseworkers do not question the desirability of segregating and quarantining individuals with communicable diseases for the protection of the larger community. The client is not free to accept or reject treatment. He must be treated. It is a definite limitation to his self-determination. The caseworker, accepting that fact, can help the patient undergo voluntary treatment and can help him work out the personality conflicts and other causal factors which brought about the problem.[70]

Question: Can a client in a public welfare agency exercise any self-determination in the midst of the agency's insistence on proof of need, on eligibility investigation and follow-up?[71]

Answer: Eligibility requirements have been established by law and must be observed by both caseworker and the client. This constitutes a legitimate limitation to the client's right to self-determination. Once his eligibility is established, however, there is no reason why the client should be deprived of any rights to self-management and self-direction.[72]

Question: How is the principle of self-determination to be applied to casework with adolescents?

Answer: Adolescents, ambivalently shifting from much self-assertion to infantile dependency, frequently need the support of parent substitutes. The caseworker may have to play a much more active role than with an adult. It must be a delicately balanced activity, on the one hand giving advice, warning and preventing injurious reality situations, while on the other hand, guarding against too much direction, avoiding the acceptance of too much dependence, and helping the adolescent assume more and more responsibility for himself.[73]

In summary, five positions regarding the principle of client self-determination existed in this decade. There was, as could be expected, some overlapping in these points of view.

The first was the position of most of the writers who stressed the importance of the principle, exhorted its implementation as the only acceptable "professional" stance, attempted to specify the activities and the role of the caseworker that accorded with the principle, and struggled to resolve the questions and problems that arose from its application.

The second position was represented by the growing number of "psychiatric" social workers, especially in the child guidance clinics, and near the end of the decade, of prestigious private family agencies which provided counseling services with noneconomic problems. They supplied the principal leadership in searching psychiatry for knowledge applicable to social work. Very early they saw that in dealing with emotional problems in interpersonal relationships, treatment plans could not be imposed. The complexity and individuality of each situation required the full involvement of the client in every phase of the casework process, and especially in treatment. The principle of client self-determination was considered to be therapeutically indispensable.

Next was the stance of many social workers in public assistance agencies who employed the principle as an expedient to reduce their own enormous caseloads that resulted from the depression. By delegating much to the client they discovered, with experience, that the principle "worked" with many clients, principally with those who were economically dependent for the first time in their lives. They also sensed the benefits accruing to their clients in non-tangible ways, such as the retaining of their sense of self-esteem and personal dignity in unpropitious circumstances.

The fourth group was those caseworkers who were disproportionately impressed by the emphasis on the casework relationship and often practiced it in an inappropriate and exaggerated manner. They pushed client self-determination to an extreme that was labeled "dynamic passivity." Gordon Hamilton referred to this practice as "silly." They conceived of their function as simply "mirroring" the client's communcation; they practically rejected study, diagnosis, and treatment planning. It was, as viewed in retrospect, the equivalent of refusing service.

The final position was manifested by caseworkers who continued to dominate and grossly manipulate clients. The reasons, implied more than expressed, were many: some caseworkers were poorly prepared professionally; some felt that client self-determination was all right for private agencies but not for public assistance agencies; some thought that it was a refinement created by impractical idealists. The caseworkers who fell into this category severely damaged the public image and reputation of social work by their manner of dealing with clients in establishing the eligibility of welfare recipients and in the periodic home visits. The social work profession ever since that time has striven to rid itself of the "snooper" reputation. It still suffers in the 1970s from the shoddy practice of some caseworkers in the days of the depression.

In this decade casework was defined as a process of helping the client "to adjust to his environment." And the depression made the environment a hostile place. Helping people to survive in these circumstances was a big enough job for social workers. Not until the 1960s was the goal of social work redefined as "the enhancement of social functioning," which was conceived as a broader and more positive purpose. If any one term could validly describe the predominant emphasis of this decade, it might be the term "reality." The harsh depression environment was a reality; securing the basic necessities of food, clothing, and shelter for millions of unemployed was a reality in terms of elementary survival. The norm, the criterion, used by many social workers in solving everyday problems of practice was the question: is it realistic? It was also, with some exceptions and qualifications mentioned above, the norm in applying the principle of client self-determination.

ENDNOTES FOR CHAPTER 2

1 John A. Fitch, "The Responsibility of Social Work in an Economic Crisis," *The Family*, April 1931, p. 50; Helen V. White, "Case Work Challenged," *The Family*, April 1931, p. 60; Baird Middaugh, "After Unemployment Publicity—What," *The Family*, April 1931, p. 73; Florence T. Waite, "What Has Been Happening?," *The Family*, April 1931, p. 142; Dorothy Roberts, "Two Interviews," *The Family*, April 1933, p. 53; Julie Stuart Driscoll, "Are We Doing Casework," *The Family*, November 1933, p. 235.
2 Blythe W. Francis, "Gains and Losses," *The Family*, March 1934, p. 8.

3 Frank H. McLean, "Progress in Adversity—1932," *The Family*, November 1932, p. 221.
4 Eleanor Neustaedter, "The Social Case Worker and Industrial Depression," *The Family*, January 1931, pp. 275-77.
5 Helen Wallerstein, "New Trends in Case Work As Developed by the Depression," *The Family*, November 1937, pp. 208-09.
6 Bertha C. Reynolds, *Between Client and Community* (Northampton Association: Smith College School of Social Work, 1934), p. 5.
7 Ibid., pp. 6, 8.
8 Ibid., p. 6.
9 Wallerstein, "New Trends in Case Work As Developed by the Depression," p. 209.
10 McLean, "Progress in Adversity—1932," p. 221; Helen Prescott Churchward, "An Experiment in Client Participation," *The Family*, April, 1936, pp. 43-48; Crystal M. Potter, "The Use of Authoritative Approach in Social Case Work," *The Family*, March 1938, pp. 19-20; Elizabeth H. Dexter, "Has Case Work a Place in the Administration of Public Relief?," *The Family*, July 1935, p. 135.
11 Virginia P. Robinson, *A Changing Psychology in Social Case Work* (Chapel Hill: University of North Carolina Press, 1930), p. 114.
12 Eleanor Neustaedter, "The Role of the Case Worker in Treatment," *The Family*, July 1932, p. 1956; Fern Lowry, "Case Work Skills and Fundamental Human Needs," *The Family*, July 1933, p. 267.
13 Reynolds, *Between Client and Community*.
14 Ibid., p. 37.
15 Bertha C. Reynolds, "A Changing Psychology in Social Case Work—After One Year," *The Family*, June 1932, p. 107.
16 Ibid.; Robinson, *A Changing Psychology in Social Case Work*, p. 184.
17 Reynolds, *Between Client and Community*, p. 7.
18 Robinson, *A Changing Psychology in Social Case Work*, p. 184.
19 Elizabeth Dexter, "Activity in Case Work Relationship," *The Family*, October 1933, pp. 203-07.
20 Gordon Hamilton, "Basic Concepts in Social Case Work," *The Family*, July 1937, p. 150.
21 Reynolds, *Between Client and Community*, p. 35; Hamilton, "Basic Concepts in Social Case Work," p. 148; Harriet M. Bartlett, "Emotional Elements in Illiness: Responsibilities of the Medical Social Worker," *The Family*, April 1940, pp. 42-43.
22 Marjorie Boggs, "Present Trends in the Case Worker's Role in Treatment," *The Family*, July 1932, p. 159; Laura A. Merrill, "The Case Worker's Role in Treatment," *The Family*, July 1932, p. 156; Grace F. Marcus, "Social Case Work and Mental Health," *The Family*, June 1938, pp. 102-05.

23 Fern Lowry, "Objectives in Social Case Work," *The Family*, December 1937, pp. 265-67; Reynolds, *Between Client and Community*, p. 116; K. Kasanin, "A Critique of Some of the Newer Trends in Case Work," *The Family*, April 1935, p. 38; Clare M. Tousley, "Case Work Principles in Interpretation," *The Family*, July 1936, p. 174; Bertha C. Reynolds, "The Things That Cannot Be Shaken," *The Family*, April 1932, pp. 53-54.

24 Driscoll, "Are We Doing Casework," p. 236.

25 Florence Hollis, "Some Contributions of Therapy to Generalized Case Work Practice," *The Family*, February 1935, p. 332.

26 Neustaedter, "The Role of the Case Worker in Treatment," pp. 152-56; Dexter, "Activity in the Casework Relationship," pp. 203-07.

27 Driscoll, "Are We Doing Casework," p. 236; Anna Budd Ware, "Family Agencies' Responsibility and Practice during an Unemployment Period," *The Family*, February 1932, pp. 302-03.

28 Lowry, "Objectives in Social Case Work," pp. 265-67.

29 Dexter, "Activity in the Casework Relationship," pp. 203-07.

30 Bertha C. Reynolds, "Can Case Closing Be Planned as a Part of Treatment?" *The Family*, July 1931, p. 142.

31 Ibid.

32 Dexter, "Activity in the Casework Relationship," pp. 203-07.

33 Ibid.; Reynolds, "Changing Psychology in Social Work—After One Year," pp. 107-11; Dexter, "Activity in the Casework Relationship," p. 203; Neustaedter, "The Role of the Case Worker in Treatment," pp. 152-56.

34 Lowry, "Objectives in Social Case Work," pp. 265-67; Dexter, "Activity in the Case Work Relationship," p. 203; Driscoll, "Are We Doing Casework," p. 236.

35 Robinson, *A Changing Psychology in Social Case Work*, pp. 164, 188.

36 Bartlett, "Emotional Elements in Illness," pp. 42-43.

37 Lowry, "Case Work Skills and Fundamental Human Needs," *The Family*, July 1933, pp. 162-63.

38 White, "Case Work Challenged," p. 60.

39 Bartlett, "Emotional Elements in Illness," pp. 42-43.

40 Neustaedter, "The Role of the Case Worker in Treatment," pp. 152-156; Dexter, "Activity in the Case Work Relationship," p. 135.

41 Bertha C. Reynolds, "The Things That Cannot Be Shaken," *The Family*, April 1932, pp. 53-54.

42 Neustaedter, "The Role of the Case Worker in Treatment," p. 152.

43 Hamilton, "Basic Concepts in Social Case Work," pp. 148-50.

44 Neustaedter, "The Role of the Case Worker in Treatment," pp. 152-56.

45 Gordon Hamilton, "Case Work Responsibility in the Unemployment Relief Agency," *The Family*, July 1934, pp. 137-38.

46 Crystal M. Potter and Lucille Nickel Austin, "The Use of the Authoritative Approach in Social Case Work," *The Family*, March 1938, pp. 19-22.
47 Ibid., p. 19.
48 Ibid., p. 22.
49 Ibid., pp. 19-22; Alice W. Rue, "The Case Work Approach to Protective
Work," *The Family*, December 1937, pp. 279-80.
50 Potter and Austin, "Use of the Authoritative Approach," p. 23.
51 Hamilton, "Basic Concepts in Social Casework," p. 148; Lucille Nickel
Austin, "Some Notes about Case Work in Probation Agencies," *The
Family*, December 1937, pp. 282-85.
52 Reynolds, *Between Client and Community*, pp. 14-15.
53 Potter and Austin, "Use of the Authoritative Approach," pp. 22-24.
54 Reynolds, *Between Client and Community*, p. 11; Emily Mitchell Wires,
"The Application of Case Work Theory to Public Welfare Practice,"
The Family, April 1936, pp. 39-42.
55 Reynolds, *Between Client and Community*, pp. 10, 25.
56 Ware, "Family Agencies' Responsibility," pp. 302-03; Reynolds,
"A Changing Psychology in Social Case Work—After One Year,"
pp. 111-12.
57 Florence R. Day, "Social Case Work and Social Adjustment," *The
Family*, October 1936, pp. 197-204.
58 Ibid., p. 199.
59 Potter and Austin, "Use of the Authoritative Approach," pp. 22-24.
60 Hamilton, "Basic Concepts in Social Case Work," pp. 148-50; Reynolds,
Between Client and Community, pp. 9-10.
61 Reynolds, *Between Client and Community*, p. 37.
62 Ibid., pp. 37-39.
63 Ibid., p. 40.
64 Ibid., pp. 41-43.
65 Potter and Austin, "Use of the Authoritative Approach," pp. 21-24.
66 Francis H. McLean, "The Case Work Laboratory," *The Family*, May
1934, pp. 90-92.
67 Anna Harrison, "Understanding the Significance of Eye Troubles," *The
Family*, February 1937, pp. 329-30.
68 Reynolds, *Between Client and Community*, pp. 106-07.
69 Eleanor Cockerill, "The Social Worker Looks at Cancer," *The Family*,
February 1937, p. 328.
70 Ruth Ellen Lindenberg, "Possibilities for Case Work Help in a Syphilis
Clinic," *The Family*, May 1939, pp. 87-90.
71 Wires, "Application of Case Work Theory," pp. 39-42.
72 Potter and Austin, "Use of the Authoritative Approach," pp. 19-22.
73 Donaldine Dudley, "Case Work Treatment of Cultural Factors in Adolescent Problems," *The Family*, December 1939, p. 249.

——————————— Social service to war casualties; shift from economic to emotional problems ——— Theory ——— Rankian psychology ———————Practice in various settings ————————————————————

CHAPTER 3

1940—1949

SINCE SOCIAL WORK exists to meet the needs of the community, what it does and how it does it are affected by domestic and world events and problems. To deal with the problems of the depression in the previous decade, untested methods had to be used, unseasoned personnel had to be absorbed, supervisory responsibility had to be delegated to staff members before they were ready for it, and as a result of emergencies that could not be controlled, some of the ideals of practice had to be compromised.

After the depression social work hoped to have a period when it could reflect upon itself, its strengths and weaknesses, expand its knowledge base, refine its skills, review its training of personnel, and standardize its professional education.[1] Social work did get a respite, but an inadequate one, lasting no more than four years. The peace was shattered by terrible wars, hot and cold.

On September 1, 1939 Germany invaded Poland and World War II began. Even though the United States did not declare war until a few years later a dark foreboding gripped the nation. It became a predominant anxiety for most Americans, including the social work profession.

> News of the war in Europe fills the minds of all of us. Many of the speakers at the National Conference integrated some reference to it with their discussions. In conversations one often heard people saying, "It's hard to think about anything but the war; everything we do and talk about seems so futile and unimportant in comparison." The emotions stirred by war are the deepest, most fundamental fears of life. . . .[2]

On December 7, 1941, Japanese planes attacked United States airfields in Hawaii and the navy ships in Pearl Harbor. The allied invasion of Normandy took place on June 6, 1944. On August 6, 1945 the United States dropped an atomic bomb on Hiroshima and on Nagasaki three days later. On May 7, 1945 Germany surrendered. Then on September 2 Japan followed.

The United States Military force, at its peak, numbered about 12,300,000; 291,557 died and many other hundreds of thousands were wounded and maimed.

The hot war was followed by the cold war. Relations with Russia, a former ally, became severely strained. Charges were made that Russian diplomatic officials stationed in the United States were used for widespread espionage in securing classified information regarding atomic fission. A wave of anti-Communism swept the country.

These events affected the life of everyone, but especially military personnel and their families. Many families suffered disruption because of dead or crippled sons and husbands.

Social work was summoned to contribute its services to the victims at home and abroad. But it found that the dominant problems of clients changed from financial and material needs of the unemployed of the depression to various types of emotional disturbances.

Now, in the war period, the complexion of the public agency case load changes. The problem of unemployment practically disappears and the reasons for needing public assistance become increasingly complicated ones, rooted in physical, psychosomatic, or other emotional disturbances, problems of old age and social or mental deterioration. Many of these cases may not be treatable; many others are, but will require unusual skill and understanding on the part of the social worker.[3]

The social work profession felt that it was inadequately prepared to deal with the emotional problems of the multitudes that needed this type of service. In the previous decade social work had begun to incorporate portions of psychiatry into its body of knowledge and skills, but it was just that—a beginning. And this was done principally by social workers in child guidance clinics and in a relatively few family agencies. Now, it felt the full impact of the meagerness of its knowledge and skill with emotional problems. Again, it had to place on many caseworkers therapeutic responsibilities for which little or no training had been provided.

The social work profession could have stood up at this time and addressed the nation, saying: "You have dumped into our laps a multitude of war victims with very serious emotional problems for which we have inadequate competence. Why don't you assign this task to some other profession?" But it did not, knowing that the number of psychiatrists at that time was insufficient to handle the problem, and knowing that no other profession existed that could undertake the responsibility. The hard fact was that if social workers would not, no one would.

If social work had refused, it would have saved itself from the following two headaches that resulted from its acceptance of the responsibility. The first was a growing negative criticism of social work by the general public. This criticism, as mentioned in the previous chapter, originated during the depression when caseworkers in public welfare agencies were accused of being snoopers, of prying into people's lives, and of pushing people around.

The negative appraisal of social work in the popular mind is wide-spread and seriously limits the services we should be in a position to render if community understanding of casework and confidence in it were greater. That there is much criticism of social work and social workers, some of it justified, but much of it not, is easily demonstrated. Not only do novels, such as *The Triumph of Willie Pond*, caricature social workers, but unflattering statements about them are not infrequent in every day life.

I had been prepared for a lack of understanding, or lack of interest in casework, but I was not prepared for the misunderstanding and active resentment and hostility that I found . . . . [4]

These censures increased during this decade and another charge was added: "They never do anything for people; their services are useless." This latter criticism was directed primarily to social workers dealing with emotional problems. The critics evidently expected to see visible, tangible "cures"; they did not, perhaps could not, appreciate the realistic but limited goals which social work set for itself: helping the client express feelings, supporting the client in difficult and depressing situations, clarifying and disentangling complex feelings. These activities were directed toward helping the client live with emotional problems. The removal of them—the curing of them—was an unrealistic expectation. But the public seemed to expect it, and when it did not occur, the charge was thrown: "What do you people do? Just talk?"

The criticism was deeply felt by caseworkers because it was loud and angry. It hurt because caseworkers were aware of their inadequate psychiatric knowledge and skills and they sometimes wondered if the criticisms were not justified. They could not simply label the critics as uninformed or bigoted. At this time lectures and workshops on psychiatric subjects were extremely popular. Any meeting hall could be filled if the announced topic contained the words "psychiatric," "emotional," or "Freud." Caseworkers were exerting efforts to fill their knowledge and skill gaps, but not effectively enough to satisfy their critics.

The second problem arising from social work's agreement to offer casework services to people with emotional disturbances was largely intramural. Some social workers vehemently contended that caseworkers should remain *social* workers and hence help the client principally and perhaps exclusively in his social adjustment. To be aware of the feelings and emotions insofar as they affected the social adjustment was proper, but it was improper to deal with the emotional problems themselves. They added that the causative factors of emotional disturbances inevitably led to the unconscious, and the unconscious definitely was the domain not of social workers but of psychiatrists. Other social workers, equally vehement, insisted that since most of the clients had emotional disturbances and needed help in their personal adjustment, caseworkers could and should acquire the necessary skills, under the guidance and supervision of the psychiatrists, to meet the need. This conflict also involved discussions about the relationship between the caseworker and the psychiatrist, and the differences between casework and psychotherapy.[5] It was at this time that the term "the poor man's psychiatrist" was first applied to caseworkers. Another controversial question that was raised was whether or not personal psychiatric analysis should be required for membership in the American Association of Psychiatric Social Workers. The requirement was not adopted, but just the consideration of it contributed to the divisiveness. These problems really caused no harm in the long run, and they helped to redefine the casework function, but for a while they disturbed the social work profession.

Such, in brief, were the disquieting conditions which colored the casework history between 1940 and 1949. Since the focal point of this book is the principle of client self-determination, it will be necessary, for the sake of clarity, to prescind as much as possible from the political tumult of the period. As the chapter unfolds, this era may appear in some phases as placid as the 1920 to 1929 decade; at other times the confusion will come within hearing distance; on a few occasions, the full impact of the troublesome times will be felt.

THEORY

The theory of client self-determination in this decade was enhanced by (1) the nation's focus on liberty and human dignity and worth, the cause for which the war was said to be fought, and (2) the psychology of the nature of man as proposed by the Functional approach to casework. The levels of the influence, quite obviously, were disparate in scope; one was rather general, the other more specific.

In the American view at the time, the basic human value that was endangered by the totalitarian governments of Nazism, Facism, and Communism was the essential dignity and worth of the human person. In totalitarianism the welfare of the state superseded the welfare of the individual. The person had only those rights that the state granted him. Personal freedom, as understood in the democracies, was abrogated.

When the totalitarian governments militarily invaded other nations and attempted to impose this political philosophy on them, wars were declared. The emotions of people in the democracies were exacerbated as news was received about the enslavement of nations and the efforts to exterminate some ethnic and religious groups. People in the United States felt that the basic issues in the war were freedom and the dignity and worth of each individual. This was why they committed to war twelve million people and the resources of the nation. This was, according to the administration and political pundits of the communication media, what it was all about.

Social workers, just as the general population, "rediscovered" the importance of the value of human dignity and worth. Theoretically it was a value known throughout the ages; its history coincided with recorded history. But World War II demonstrated the disastrous results of a nation or a group of nations that denied it in practice.

Social workers recognized anew that the value of the human person was, and had to be, the supreme value of the profession, and that the principle of client self-determination was the first and immediate consequence of it. Gordon Hamilton expressed it succinctly: "Under the philosophy of self-determination of the client, practice . . . must spring from respect for the essential dignity of human beings."[6] Other writers spoke similarly.[7]

What happened was this: the principle of client self-determination was placed into the context of the supreme value, a more inclusive and comprehensive framework. It no longer stood alone. The association of the two concepts and the more accurate relationship of the two would have practical consequences in the succeeding decades. For instance, in 1960 Saul Bernstein, sensing that the principle of client self-determination was being inappropriately used by some social workers, raised an important question, which was the title of his article: "Self-Determination: King or Citizen in the Realm of Values?" His conclusion was:

> While self-determination is not supreme, it is supremely important. Only through the rich utilization of this concept can we fully honor the human-worth value. This is in line with the best in democratic traditions.[8]

The relationship between these two values will also help guide social workers through the Scylla and Charybdis implicit in "aggressive casework," "reaching out," "parenting" and other direct interventive methods which will come to the fore in the next decade.

The second influence that enhanced the theory of client self-determination was psychological. It came from the theory of personality of the Functional approach to social work. For a while it was considered another disruptive development, a vexatious schism.

Before its appearance, caseworkers seemed to agree on the principles of casework; after it appeared, there were two "schools," the Diagnostic and the Functional. Although the fundamental differences between the two approaches have never been fully reconciled, and they probably never will be (in the meantime other approaches have been added: the problem-solving and the behavioral modification), the Functional exerted a notable influence on the theory of casework and specifically on the principle of client self-determination.

As mentioned in the previous chapter, it began in the 1930s in the School of Social Work of the University of Pennsylvania. Based on a theory of personality provided by Otto Rank, and developed by Jessie Taft and Virginia Robinson, its basic concepts were well defined by 1950. In that year Cora Kasius, editor of *Social Casework* published *A Comparison of the Diagnostic and Functional Casework Concepts,*[9] which delineated the similarities and differences of the basic assumptions in the two approaches.

The three areas of the Functional approach that differentiated it from the Diagnostic concerned the nature of man, the purpose of casework, and the concept of practice.[10]

Concerning the nature of man, Rank's contributions "were in such areas as the nature of human growth, the human self— with particular emphasis on the will as a controlling and organizing force—the way psychological help can be given and taken through relationship. . . ."[11] This was quite a different psychological base from the Diagnostic approach built upon a Freudian foundation. The Functionalists considered the latter as a "somewhat mechanistic, deterministic view of man, which saw him for the most part prey to the dark forces of an unconscious and of the harsh restricted influences of parental dicta in the early years of growth."[12]

In the Functional theory of the nature of man a new respect for man and his potentialities was fundamental. Man was not just the product of uncontrolled forces; he had creative abilities. The existence of a "will" was postulated; it was conceived as a "controlling and organizing force." The client in casework, then, was offered a relationship through which his own powers of choice and growth could be released.

The Functional group did not dispute the existence and influence of environmental influences, of irrational impulses, and of the unconscious. It did not deny the need for intervention and treatment of emotional disturbances by psychiatrists. But it chose to direct its "helping" method toward the inner potential for growth and purposive, constructive activity which, it was convinced, every person had. The result of the helping process was not the "treatment" planned by the caseworker, but the self-direction and self-control of the client in the modification of himself, his relationships, and his environment.

The effect of this approach upon the principle of client self-determination was obvious. It offered a theory for the foundation of the principle. The importance of self-determination, according to this orientation, was placed in the very nature of man; and that was why it was a civic right in a democratic society, why it was a psychological need, and why it was necessary for effectiveness in social work.

In the years to come, the Diagnostic approach to casework would gradually soften the assumptions of classical Freudianism about the nature of man and develop an Ego Psychology, which would be considerably more optimistic about man's potentialities. It is hard to deny the influence of the Functional approach on this development.

But, in this decade of the 40s, the Functional school was considered by some social workers a disrupter of the unity of casework.

In 1941 Gordon Hamilton felt safe in enumerating the points of a common foundation of all casework, principles upon which the two approaches to casework rested. She recognized the differences between the Diagnostic and Functional orientations, but was convinced that the basic essentials of casework were acceptable to both orientations.

> When I say that in casework we are now facing divergence, I must remind you that we hold the above as a sound foundation so that we can perhaps tolerate discussion of what is unlike without too much frustration.[13]

In 1947 Kenneth L. M. Pray denied that there was a common base in casework. The differences which Gordon Hamilton thought were nonessential, insisted Mr. Pray, were essential.

> . . . there was a time not long ago when it would have been fairly easy to enumerate a set of generic principles that practically all social case workers would have accepted as forming the founda-

tions of their own practice. . . . It is not easy—indeed, it seems to me impossible—to make such a list today. Genuine and substantial differences of viewpoint have appeared, concerning not only what is truly basic and essential in social casework practice but even what actually constitutes social casework practice itself. . . .[14]

In 1950 Cora Kasius, in her book comparing the two approaches, made a statement which, if accepted by the profession as valid, meant the end of unity on casework fundamentals:

> Because of the nature and profundity of the differences in philosophy, purpose, and method, the committee is in agreement in believing that these two orientations cannot be effectively reconciled or combined.[15]

In 1950 Gordon Hamilton wrote a book review of Kasius' book and expressed an anxiety she did not have in 1941. Her words seemed to indicate that she suppressed a great deal more apprehension than she permitted herself to verbalize.

> The conceptual differences are indeed striking, and while one can only be relieved to have them brought out, the implications for social work education and for the profession as a whole are grave. In the healthy growth of any profession differences and experiment are to be assumed, but the nature of *these* differences and the unlikelihood of their reconciliation must now be realistically faced by many agencies and schools which have evaded the issue or hoped for some measure of integration.[16]

Time, fortunately, demonstrated that the fears of Hamilton did not materialize. The existence of two approaches did not disintegrate casework. Both approaches profited from each other.

In this decade there were many references to client self-determination, and a few articles appeared on the philosophy,[17] the principles,[18] and the evolution[19] of casework, all of which devoted a few paragraphs or pages to it, but not one wrote a full article on the principle of client self-determination. When these many references are collated, they can be woven into the following statements which serve as a general description of the principle as understood at this time.

1. The concept of client self-determination is opposed to the exercise of an authoritative reformist role by the caseworker, wherein things are "done to" the client and wherein the caseworker imposes his own goals, solutions, standards of behavior, and morals upon the client.[20]

2. The concept of client self-determination is based on the following beliefs: (a) that human personality has inherent strengths and powers for growth and change; (b) that clients have a *right* to solve their problems in their own way and to make their own decisions and plans; (c) that clients have a *need* to have this right recognized and respected in the casework helping situation; and (d) that this right and need are common to all persons, to the poor and less fortunate as well as to the "socially successful."[21]

3. Casework, therefore, helps the client to clarify, stimulate, and activate the client's potentialties for self-help, self-reliance, and self-direction by helping him use the available and appropriate resources of the community and of his own personality. Casework denies any "pat answers in the back of the book" and refrains from exerting strong influences or pressures on the client's will.[22]

Comparing this general statement to the one in the previous decades, the notable advance in theory is the greater emphasis upon the client: his strengths and potentialities, his right and need for self-determination. This apparently resulted from the prominence given to the value of human dignity and worth in the nation during the war period. As for the role of the caseworker, not much of anything new was added to the general theory. But there was considerable discussion of the role of the caseworker in the various settings in which casework was practiced.

PRACTICE

Casework deals not with the person-in-the-abstract, with generalized strengths, weaknesses, and needs, but with a specific person, very individual in most instances, including the problem for which he seeks help. These factors complicate the application of the principle of client self-determination in practice. The literature of this decade, however, did not merely say that the principle must be individualized on a case-to-case basis. It attempted to go further by explicating it on a setting-to-setting basis.

1. *In a Medical Setting.* "Medical Setting" is not a univocal term; it may have as many different meanings as "physical illness." The caseworker, being a member of the team in a hospital, clinic, or institution, derives a portion of her function from the general function of the team. This, in turn, depends upon the patient's type of illness.

 • *With surgical patients,* who are confronted with the decision of undergoing an operation, the function of the caseworker should be (a) to acquire an understanding of the various medical, social, and emotional factors concerning the patient's illness, his personality, and his social background; (b) to help the patient understand the recommendations of the medical authority; and (c) to help the patient make his own decision.

> A recommendation for surgery frequently leaves the patient confused, bewildered, and apprehensive. He is faced by the necessity of deciding what to do about it. Often he is both afraid to have the operation and afraid to risk the consequences of not having it. Frequently, the caseworker is asked to help the patient reach a decision or to work out a solution for some of the problems associated with admission to the hospital. It is important that the final decision be the patient's own and that the responsibility for either accepting or rejecting the recommendation remain with him. However, our desire to have him assume this responsibility may limit our helpfulness to him unless we have some real understanding of how we, as caseworkers, can really enable him to function. Dr. Michaels has emphasized the importance of recognizing the influence of five factors (purpose and type of the operation, structure and organization of the personality, psycho-sexual development, age, and organ involved) upon the patient's reactions to surgery.[23]

 • *With patients suffering from a disability,* such as a rheumatic heart or tuberculosis, the function of the caseworker should be to promote the patient's adherence to the prescribed medical program, to help him understand and work through his own specific problems in relation to the illness, and to aid him in accepting the disability realistically.

> There has been a constant war against tuberculosis. In its earlier stages this fight was on a mechanical level of cleaning up slums, taking mass X-rays, or providing the proper type of hospital care. But now we have come to realize that it is a human being that is the subject of all this attention, and the control of the disease will come only when the sick person is ready to participate in the treatment process. And to assist in this the medical social worker assumes his place in the treatment team.[24]

● *With patients suffering from a contagious disease,* such as the venereally infected, a more direct role was advised; for instance, an active direction of the patient; a supportive and protective service; and helping the patient release tensions, lessen anxieties, and clarify the situation by helping the patient to talk about his disturbance.

> Social agencies need to evaluate their methods of handling this type of patient. The writers believe that social agencies need to assume a more active role in following up the patient and that a case should not be closed without some effort at actively directing the girl. The social agency services, in many instances, will take on a protective aspect. . . .[25]

The principle of self-determination in a medical setting recognized two types of limitations: a voluntarily accepted medical authority and a legal health ordinance.

In most instances a person was free to accept or reject medical services. But, if he freely accepted surgery or medicinal treatment, he entered into a quasi contract to cooperate with the treatment plan. He voluntarily accepted the authority of the medical service and agreed to follow the regimen it prescribed. The patient created the medical authority in the sense that it would have no power over him if he had not voluntarily accepted its services. Therefore, when a caseworker helped the patient to adhere to the medical program, he was helping the patient accomplish the patient's own freely made decision.

In a few instances, such as with contagious diseases, civil law demanded treatment, principally for the protection of other people. And civil law was recognized as a legitimate limitation of human freedom.

2. *With Unmarried Mothers*. At least three different attitudes were expressed in the casework literature in regard to the caseworker's function in this setting. All three agreed that the caseworker should help the mother clarify realistically the various aspects of the problem and acquaint her with the available alternatives from which she could choose. The first, however, insisted that the mother *alone* make the final decision of giving up or keeping the child; the second maintained that the *worker should actively participate* in the final decision; and the third attitude directed the caseworker to take a *more active "steering" role* in helping the mother make a good decision. The third attitude differed from the second in the *degree* of responsibility that the worker assumed and the degree of pressure which the caseworker exerted upon the client to arrive at a certain decision.

• *According to the first attitude*, the function of the caseworker was (a) to help the mother gain an understanding of her feelings by giving her an opportunity to tell her problems in her own way; (b) to aid the mother in facing her situation realistically by considering all the ramifications of her problem, her own needs and the child's, both for the present and for the future; (c) to assist the mother in seeing the various possibilities and alternatives of handling the problem and the facilities and resources available; and (d) to give the mother an opportunity to use her strengths in working out a plan for the child and herself, and to give the mother support in the plan she finally adopts.

> The caseworker's goal is to help a mother plan for her child so that both of them will fulfill happy, useful lives. If the plan ultimately decided upon by the mother does not seem to offer the child the opportunity for optimum growth and happiness, the caseworker must, nevertheless, still abide by that decision since the mother has every right to her child.[26]

• *According to the second attitude,* most unmarried mothers were considered to be serious neurotics who did not have the capacity to make a realistic decision without the active participation of the caseworker. Therefore, the caseworker made an evaluation of the mother and of the alternatives, and helped the mother choose the most realistic and practical one. The caseworker did not coerce, but tried to save the mother from adopting a plan that was inevitably doomed to failure.

> Most unmarried mothers are serious neurotics, and one of the most prevalent symptoms of a neurosis is an inability to make and act upon conscious decisions based on the reality situation. How can we rationally expect the neurotic unmarried mother to make a realistic decision if we leave the total burden to her? In reality the caseworker cannot escape the responsibility for participating actively in this decision.[27]

• *According to the third attitude,* the caseworker took an active "steering" role to help the mother make a good decision for herself and the child; she "took sides" about the plan and aligned herself with what she believed to be the best decision. The caseworker did not coerce, but exerted pressure upon the client to choose the plan which the caseworker considered best.

> In helping the client to discover and work through emotional needs, the caseworker should take sides by pointing out those elements that make it desirable or undesirable to keep the child. She may go a step further by aligning herself openly with the healthier part of the client's personality and state what she believes to be the best decision.[28]

Caseworkers representing these three attitudes were struggling with the following underlying issues. Is the unmarried mother, because of her problem, really capable of responsible decision making? Does the caseworker have the responsibility to prevent the mother from deciding on a plan that the caseworker thought to be unwise? Does the mother alone have the right to decide the child's destiny? Does the child have rights, and if so, is the caseworker a protector of the rights of the child? The stand taken on these issues affected the caseworker's understanding and implementation of the principle of client self-determination.

3. *In a Probation or Parole Agency.* The casework literature did not contain much discussion of *how* the probation or parole officer could help the client choose, decide, and act freely. The questions discussed were these. Is there *any* area in which the probationer or parolee is self-determining? Are there *any* non-authoritative aspects in the relationship between the caseworker and the client in this setting? The literature did not advance much beyond these questions.

The actual wording of the problem was phrased more broadly: is casework *possible* in a probation and parole agency? The compatibility of three concepts in casework with the authority of the agency was questioned: the concept of "acceptance," the "non-judgmental attitude," and the principle of client self-determination. What the literature said about all three could be applied with equal validity to each. David Dressler raised the pertinent questions very clearly.

> Is parole a casework function? If so, how are casework techniques and philosophy adapted to the parole process? Considering the setting of any parole agency, is casework possible?[29]

> Probation and parole organizations particularly have a knotty problem to solve with respect to the amalgam of casework and legal dicta. What can and should a worker do in an authoritarian agency? How far be authoritarian? How far non-judgmental?[30]

• *According to the first opinion,* good casework principles can be employed, and further, the proper use of authority can facilitate intensive therapy with an individual.[31] Two areas need to be recognized. In the first, the authority of the agency determines rules and regulations that the client must obey. Certain conditions are stipulated and certain behaviors are forbidden. In this area client self-determination is limited by law; actually it is a relatively narrow sphere. In the second area, which encompasses all the rest of the client's life that is not governed by legal restrictions, which is an immeasurably larger area, the client has the same freedom that any person enjoys.[32]

• *According to the second opinion,* casework is practically impossible because the client simply does not have the security to act upon the distinction expressed in the first opinion. The client knows that his probation officer is an officer of the court. He does not feel secure to discuss openly and realistically sensitive areas of his life with a person who has such power over him. He simply cannot see one and the same person as an officer of the court and as a therapist. The client feels that he must present himself to the probation officer in the most favorable light.[33] In brief, in this setting clients generally do not feel free to enter into a casework relationship.

4. *In a Public Assistance Agency.* Although the public image of social workers in a public assistance agency was a poor one, because they were accused of "pushing people around," the statements in the literature of this decade about client self-determination in this setting were clear and positive. In brief, the client had to fulfill the eligibility requirements, but beyond that, he had the right to determine himself fully.

> The belief that it is impossible to do casework in a public assistance agency because of the rigidity of eligibility requirements set forth in the law is both widespread and erroneous.

> It is true that the law sets forth certain basic factors of eligibility which must be met before the client can receive financial assistance from the agency .... Within these limitations of basic eligibility the worker can do case work much the same as the worker in any other agency.[34]

The caseworker's function, once eligibility has been established, was to acquaint the client with the available services and resources in the agency or the community which might be useful or helpful to him. In discussing these, the caseworker was instructed to guard against giving the client the impression that he must accept the caseworker's suggestions in order to establish or maintain his eligibility. It must be made clear that he is free to accept or reject the suggestions. Jane Hoey's statement is classical and deserves to be quoted at length.

Since the agency's effectiveness rests upon respect for the individual's integrity and recognition of his right to make his own decisions and to follow his own way of life, it can go no further than to discuss and suggest such services. The individual is free to accept or reject the suggestions without affecting his basic right to money payments. He may wish to obtain on his own initiative the services indicated—or he may feel no need for them. This is an important element of the cooperative relation between the two, and the matter may be put in these words: The agency is responsible for observing situations in which it thinks services of some kind might be useful—and for discussing these with applicant or recipient sufficiently to make the suggestions clear and to learn whether he wants to ask for or receive the services. It is bound to guard scrupulously, however, against any approach or suggestion that might lead the individual to believe that, in order to establish or maintain eligibility for financial aid, he must accept offers of services or other suggestions . . . .[35]

A specific in client self-determination was the client's freedom to spend the cash payments when and how he wished.

A cash payment is made in recognition of the fact that a client does not, by reason of financial dependence, lose his capacity to select how, when, and whether each of his requirements is to be met. In this way the client is assured of his right to use his payment with the same freedom as do persons who receive their income from other sources and to carry on his business through normal channels of exchange.[36]

If caseworkers in this setting had put into their daily practice these convictions about client self-determination, the criticisms of them would have been blunted. The usual explanations for failing in large measure to do this was that the caseworkers in public assistance agencies were inadequately trained and overburdened with huge caseloads.

5. *With Military Personnel*. During and after the war, social caseworkers were called to assist military personnel in three settings.

a. *In army posts* they functioned as assistants to psychiatrists, helping soldiers with personality problems that prevented their adjustment to military life. The treatment goals were specific and limited.

> The treatment goals, however, had to be limited to meeting specific situations and to achieving adjustments to definite assignments. The social workers were not treating the basic causes of maladjustment. They were concerned with the problems of why the patient was forced to use personality deficiencies as a means of adjustment and, insofar as possible, the situation that stimulated this use of illness was the focus of treatment.[37]

The technical manual issued to military psychiatric social workers stressed the importance of the principle of client self-determination.

> In the casework process this principle of individual self-determination must be recognized. The ultimate decision belongs to the patient. He alone can determine what course of action he is to take when confronted with a specific situation. It is the function of the military psychiatric social worker to open to the patient the course of action he may take by helping him obtain correct information, a reality base for self-judgment, and by helping him to determine what resources are at his disposal.[38]

b. *In discharge centers* social workers aided veterans with their adjustment to civilian life. The veterans who were referred to social service suffered from a temporarily impaired capacity for self-determination. The military life accustomed them to taking orders, to having decisions made for them. Then upon discharge, they suddenly were expected to manage their own affairs.

> The veteran may be less ready to take positive steps alone than he was before he went into service. This may also be only temporary and in the nature of a hangover from his order-taking days in service . . . . Choice and responsibility for decisions are absent in the training camp: the average G. I. has surrendered the right of choice of lodgings, food, clothing, transportation, occupation, and companions. He has spent months alternately training furiously

and sitting or standing about waiting for the next order.

Now, with the discharge papers signed, he must begin to make not only all the little decisions of everyday civilian living, but must also, and as quickly as possible, reach some of the most momentous decisions of his entire life. It is the rare G. I. who can face all this without some insecurity, and those who work with him must be aware of this.[39]

The degree of impairment for self-determination varied among discharged veterans. In most cases, a short-term assistance was adequate. It involved reassurance, mobilization of resources, and helping with concrete needs. In some cases, where the movement from dependence to independence was more difficult, the caseworker had to be more active, involving a "doing" for the client, a modified parental role, which included guidance and direction.[40]

c. *In Veteran Hospitals* the social workers helped veterans reestablish familiar ties and return home. Generally, this was a service with the same characteristics as casework in any medical setting. In a few cases, however, the caseworkers had to employ authoritative methods with reluctant or uncooperative families in order to facilitate the veteran's discharge from the hospital.

The hospital sometimes uses considerable authority in bringing about a contact with the agency if the family does not follow up on a referral. . . . There was some early skepticism on the part of the staff when referrals carried an "or else" threat, for that was something with which they were not too familiar.[41]

6. *In Child-Placing Agencies.* The central problem in cases brought to a child-placing agency was the unsatisfactory relationship between parents and child. Casework help may have resulted in placing the child in a foster home or in helping the parents improve that relationship. Some of the parents came voluntarily and some were authoritatively referred to the agency. Two attitudes were expressed by caseworkers concerning the application of the principle of client self-determination in this setting.

a. *The first attitude* stressed parental rights. The care of children is the right of parents, and this right does not cease when problems occur. Moreover, in times of problems, the parents have the right to determine the solution.

> The primary right of the parent to his child is in essence the right of the parent to determine the ultimate solution to the conflict in his relationship to his child. Practice under this philosophy accepts the client as a responsible human being who is asking for help with a problem in his living and recognizes that he must be free to solve that problem to his own satisfaction if he is to live with that solution. The authoritative reformist role of the caseworker gives way to the concept of self-determination of the client.[42]

Since caseworkers cannot take over the responsibility of parents there must be a basic faith and trust in the ability of parents to arrive at a satisfactory solution to the problem, and a faith in their ability to bear the consequences.

> Under the philosophy of self-determination of the client, practice must therefore be rooted in an unshakable conviction of the validity of the principle; it must spring from respect for the essential dignity of human beings; it must be based on the belief that even a more or less bewildered client has the right to determine his own destiny with what case work help we have to offer; and it must have faith in his ability to bear the consequences of that right.[43]

According to this attitude, the function of the caseworker was to understand the meaning of the parent's behavior in relation to the child; to diagnose the parent's ability and desire to assume this parental responsibility; to help the parent know what placement will really mean to him and to his child; and to leave the decision to him, meanwhile holding the parent to the realities involved.

b. *The second attitude* stressed the responsibility of the caseworker for promoting *the welfare of the child*. The proposed basis for assuming greater responsibility was the caseworker's knowledge, enriched by the contributions of psychiatry, of the physical and emotional needs of children, a knowledge which presumably surpassed that of parents.

The contributions of psychiatry have vastly increased our knowledge of the basic emotional as well as physical needs of children and the damage that is done when these needs are not met. Increased knowledge brings increased concern. If we act on that concern, then all casework must recognize a more total responsibility regardless of what brings the client to the agency.[44]

In implementing this responsibility, caseworkers sometimes met with resistance from parents. Efforts were made to establish a constructive relationship with parents, to understand parental needs and problems, and to ventilate and clarify feelings. If these casework efforts were not successful, the deliberate use of authority and protective measures were employed to promote the child's welfare in both voluntary and nonvoluntary cases.[45]

7. *With the Aged*. In the literature of this decade, caseworkers expressed the conviction that advanced age, usually understood to be sixty-five or more, should not, in itself, be a limiting factor to client self-determination. The aged are not a homogeneous group; they are individuals with varying degrees of abilities to manage their own affairs. The spectrum ranges from those who are as capable of taking care of themselves as they did in the prime of life, to others who need a direct management for daily existence. In working with the aged, caseworkers must evaluate the strengths of the aged person for self-direction and be convinced of three things: "(1) The right of the aged person, as of other individuals, to self-determination. (2) The ability of the aged to achieve some degree of adjustment and growth. . . . (3) That old age is as important as any other phase of life. . . ."[46]

A further point is stressed: self-management and self-determination should be encouraged in the aged even more than in younger people. When people are younger they tend to bounce back from dependence to independence. In the case of the aged, temporary dependence upon others is more apt to lead to permanent dependence. A sense of independence is seen as a barometer of health and of the desire to live. Hence, with appropriate safeguards to prevent injury, caseworkers push and insist on the self-determination of the aged more than they do with other clients.

ENDNOTES FOR CHAPTER 3

1   Annette Garrett, "The Professional Base of Social Casework," *The Family*, July 1946, p. 167.
2   Editorial, "Case Work in a Democracy," *The Family*, July 1940, p. 165.
3   Catherine M. Manning, "Differentiated Use of Staff in a Public Agency," *The Family*, January 1943, p. 327.
4   Garrett, "Professional Base of Social Casework," p. 167.
5   Grete L. Bibring, "Psychiatry and Social Work," *Journal of Social Casework*, June 1947, pp. 205-10; Bibring, "Psychiatric Principles In Casework," *Journal of Social Casework*, June 1949, pp. 231-34; Grace F. Marcus, "Distinctions between Psychotherapy and Social Casework," *Social Work in the Current Scene* (New York: University of Columbia Press, 1949), pp. 268-81; Jules V. Coleman, "Distinguishing between Psychotherapy and Casework," *Journal of Social Casework*, June 1949, pp. 244-51.
6   Gordon Hamilton, "The Underlying Philosophy of Social Casework," *The Family*, July 1941, pp. 37-39.
7   S. Ross Pond, Letter to the Editor, *Social Casework*, April 1950, p. 166; Luna Bowdoin Brown, "Responsibility of the Public Agency for Strengthening Its Clients," *Journal of Social Casework*, July 1948, pp. 256-59; Editorial, "Case Work in a Democracy," pp. 165-66; Ruth Z.S. Mann, "The War and Case Work," *The Family*, July 1943, p. 327; Gordon Hamilton, "Helping People—the Growth of a Profession," *Journal of Social Casework*, October 1948, pp. 294-95.
8   Saul Bernstein, "Self-Determination: King or Citizen in the Realm of Values?," *Social Work*, January 1960, p. 8.
9   Cora Kasius, *A Comparison of Diagnostic and Functional Casework Concepts* (New York: Family Service Association of America, 1950), p. 13.
10 Ruth E. Smalley, "The Functional Approach to Casework Practice," *Theories of Social Casework* eds. Robert W. Roberts and Robert H. Nee (Chicago: University of Chicago Press, 1970) p. 79.
11 Ibid., p. 83.
12 Ibid., p. 82.
13 Hamilton, "Underlying Philosophy of Social Casework," pp. 139-44.
14 Kenneth L. M. Pray, "A Restatement of the Generic Principles of Social Casework Practice," *Journal of Social Casework*, October 1947, pp. 285-90.

15 Kasius, "Comparison of Diagnostic and Functional Casework Concepts," p. 13.
16 Gordon Hamilton, Book Report, *Social Casework*, October 1950, p. 343.
17 Gordon Hamilton, "Philosophy of Social Work," pp. 139-44.
18 Pray, "Generic Principles of Social Casework Practice," pp. 285-90.
19 Annette Garrett, "Historical Survey of the Evolution of Casework," *Journal of Social Casework*, June 1949, pp. 219-20.
20 Pond, Letter to the Editor, p. 166; Hamilton, "Helping People," p. 294.
21 Hertha Kraus, "The Role of Social Casework in American Social Work," *Social Casework*, January 1950, pp. 9-10.
22 Maude von P. Kemp, "The Child Welfare Service Job and the Community," *The Family*, January 1943, pp. 337-38; Hamilton, "Helping People," p. 294; Garrett, "Evolution of Casework," pp. 219-20.
23 Eleanor E. Cockerill, "Psychiatric Understanding in Social Case Work with Surgical Patients," *The Family*, February 1943, pp. 369-70.
24 Jean Berman and Leo H. Berman, "The Signing Out of Tuberculosis Patients," *The Family*, April 1944, pp. 67-73.
25 Virginia Fenske and H. L. Rachlin, "Social Redirection of Venereally Infected Women," *The Family*, May 1945, p. 115.
26 Sylvia Oshlag, "Surrendering a Child for Adoption," *The Family*, June 1945, pp. 135-44; Erma C. Blethen, "Case Work Service to a Florence Crittenton Home," *The Family*, November 1942, pp. 250-51; Ruth F. Brenner, "Case Work Service for Unmarried Mothers," *The Family*, November 1941, p. 211.
27 Leontine R. Young, "The Unmarried Mother's Decision about Her Baby," *Journal of Social Casework*, January 1947, pp. 27-31.
28 Frances H. Scherz, "'Taking Sides' in the Unmarried Mother's Conflict," *Journal of Social Casework*, February 1947, pp. 57-58.
29 David Dressler, "Case Work in Parole," *The Family*. March 1941, pp. 3-6.
30 David Dressler, "Case Work in an Authoritarian Agency," *The Family*, December 1941, pp. 276-80.
31 Stephan H. Clink and Millard Prichard, "Case Work in a Juvenile Court," *The Family*, December 1944, pp. 305-07.
32 Dressler, "Case Work in Parole," pp. 3-6.
33 Dressler, "Case Work in an Authoritarian Agency," pp. 276-80.
34 Meta L. Landuyt, "Case Work in a Public Agency," *The Family*, April 1944, pp. 43-44.
35 Jane M. Hoey, "Public Assistance in 1948," *Journal of Social Casework*, April 1948, p. 124.
36 Brown, "Responsibility of Public Agency," pp. 256-59.
37 Albert Lehman, "Short-Term Therapy in a Military Setting," *The Family*, October 1944, pp. 223-24.

38 Department of the Army, *Military Psychiatric Social Work*, Technical Manual, TM 8-241 (Washington: U. S. Government Printing Office, 1950), pp. 15-16.

39 Ethel L. Ginsburg, "The Veteran—A Challenge to Case Work," *The Family*, October 1944, p. 207.

40 Betty P. Mahaffy, "Helping the Serviceman Re-establish Parental Ties," *The Family*, July 1946, p. 187.

41 Grace F. Mayberg, "Cooperation between a Veterans Hospital and a Family Agency," *The Family*, July 1945, pp. 213-15.

42 Henrietta L. Gordon, "Discharge: An Integral Aspect of the Placement Process," *The Family*, April 1941, pp. 37-39.

43 Ibid.

44 Helen A. Wisgerhof, "Casework in Non-voluntary Referrals," *Journal of Social Casework*, November 1946, pp. 278-79.

45 Ibid.

46 Joan M. Smith, "Psychological Understanding in Casework with the Aged," *Journal of Social Casework*, May 1948, pp. 189-93.

CHAPTER 4

A 1950 DEFINITION

OF CLIENT SELF-DETERMINATION

BEFORE PROCEEDING to the next decade, it seems desirable to pause at this point. It is a natural half-way mark of this fifty-year history.

Analogically, the social work profession by 1950 evolved into young adulthood. The next two decades would see social work in its maturity, with accomplishments and successes, with frustrations and disappointments that are characteristic of full adulthood. The first three decades constitute a distinct era; it will be followed by another set of decades, another era, which, though organically related, is quite different.

In the previous chapters, the evolution of the principle of client self-determination was traced from its beginnings in American social work. The process was emphasized. Bits and pieces of thought, contributed by many social workers, were

73

gathered and discussed. Most of the components appeared in each decade, but as the years passed and as casework itself developed, new theoretical aspects and new practice insights were added. It may be useful to devote a few pages to looking at the whole, to see how the pieces add up, and to see the results of the evolutionary process.

Although there were differences of opinion on a few issues, it appears possible and desirable to formulate a common-denominator definition of the principle of client self-determination as it was understood at the end of the third decade.[1]

Up to this time, client self-determination was dicussed almost exclusively in the casework context. The application of the principle to the other social work methods was rarely found in the literature prior to 1950. So, the pages that follow reflect the casework emphasis.

In the briefest possible terms the concept of client freedom can be stated in three propositions:

1. The client has a right and a need to be free in making his own decisions and choices.

2. This right to freedom, however, is limited by the client's capacity, by law and authority, by unwritten community standards, and by the function of the agency.

3. The caseworker has a corresponding duty to respect the right, in theory and in practice, by refraining from any direct or indirect interference with it, and by positively helping the client to exercise that right.

1. *The Right and Need*. The client is a human being who seeks the services of a social agency to help him with a need or a problem. As a human being he has the responsibility of living his life in such a manner as to achieve his life's goals, proximate and ultimate, as he conceives them. Corresponding to this responsibility, he is endowed with a fundamental, inalienable right to freedom. This is the right to choose and decide the means for the prosecution of his own personal destiny.

When a client applies for the service of a social agency, the caseworker should presume that the client has no intention, under ordinary circumstances, of surrendering either his basic right to freedom or any of its derivatives. Ordinarily he has no intention of bartering his freedom, or any part of it, for the material assistance or the counseling service he receives from the agency.

He comes to a social agency because he wants assistance with a need or a problem. He believes that the social caseworker, because of her professional competence, can acquaint him with the resources in the community and within himself which can be used to meet his need and solve his problem. The client wants to know what choices are available to him, and will welcome the caseworker's evaluation of each alternative, but he wants to remain free to make his own decisions. He feels that, after he is helped to acquire the facts and after he is helped to see the full objective picture of his problem and the available means thereto, he and he alone is most competent to make the decisions. And he is fully justified in this because the decisions ordinarily concern those things which relate to his own private and home life.

Moreover, when a client freely seeks the services of a social agency, he has the right to decide whether he wants the service or treatment which the agency offers and how much of it. He is free to terminate his relationship with the agency at will.

The client needs freedom to make his own decisions in order to make the casework help effective. Caseworkers, throughout the thirty years of casework literature, have given abundant practical testimony of the futility of casework when plans are superimposed upon the client by the caseworker. Social responsibility, emotional adjustment, personality growth, and maturity are possible only when the client exercises his freedom of choice and decision.

2. *The Limitations.* The casework literature observed that limitations to personal freedom are obvious, real factors in everyday human living. Traffic regulations are a simple exam-

ple. The driver's rate of speed is limited by the city's statutes and his stopping and starting are regulated by traffic lights.

The client, as all human beings, lives in society. The other members of society also have the same basic freedoms. Each person has a right to freedom, and a corresponding duty to respect the rights of other persons. These duties, to respect the rights of others, consitute limitations to freedom.

Moreover, apart from the limitations arising from the rights of others, the basic freedom of the individual is limited in itself. Freedom is not synonymous with license. Freedom is not meant to promote rampant individualism. Freedom is a means, not a goal in itself. It is a means for attaining the person's legitimate goals in life. They include the development of his own personality and his relationship to other persons. The basic individual freedom, therefore, does not sanction self-injury nor self-destruction in any of these areas.

The limitations to the client's freedom arise from four sources: (a) his temporary incapacity to use his freedom constructively; (b) law and authority; (c) the unwritten community standards; and (d) agency function.

a. *The incapacity of the client* should not be gratuitously presumed by the caseworker. Rather, the assumption should be that the client is capable of making his own constructive plans and decisions. This assumption should be sustained until the caseworker has clear evidence, or at least a prudent doubt, concerning the client's capacity for decision-making. The incapacity of clients will have degrees. It is the function of the caseworker, then, to evaluate the degree of the client's capacity for self-determination.

Some clients will be able to keep the full responsibility for the direction of their own situation and will need help of an informational sort only. Others will be too weak to assume full responsibility in their own affairs and will need the active support of the caseworker. Temporarily, the caseworker must share some of the responsibility for making decisions in the case of some clients. This, however, must be done only to the degree that the client is incapacitated. A few clients may be so impaired in their capacity for adjustment that they need to be treated as socially sick persons. In extreme instances, in emergencies, the caseworker may have to act as quickly as an ambulance surgeon, especially in the case of the very ill or ignorant or inarticulate. But these instances may be rare, and will be accurately and instinctively recognized by the caseworker who generally follows the principle of client self-determination. Refusal to share the responsibility with such clients would be equivalent to a refusal of service.

The justification for the caseworker's active participation in helping clients to make decisions, in proportion to their incapacity, is the caseworker's social responsibility. The social function of agencies and caseworkers is generally accepted. Social agencies, even private agencies, have certain responsibilities to the community. The community's stake in casework is emphasized by the fact that it is ultimately the financial support of social agencies today. The minimum expectation of the community is that caseworkers help to protect clients from injuring themselves and others through an unregulated or illegitimate use of personal freedom.

The caseworker's active sharing in the client's decision, moreover, should be temporary; that is, only as long as the client continues to lack the full capacity for self-direction. The caseworker's evaluation of the client's capacity must be continuous, so that as soon as he regains it, the caseworker must relinquish her activity in his decisions.

In other words, the principle of client freedom, just as any other casework principle or method, should not be applied rigidly with universal sameness to every client and to every problem. Just as casework generally is individualized in accordance with the differentials of the client's personality, his needs, the function of the agency, and the setting, so also the principle of client self-determination must be individualized. The ideal of each client being fully self-determined must be modified by the realities in each individual instance.

More detailed directives for caseworkers on this point seem impossible and undesirable. The caseworker's professional equipment should include a deep respect for the client's basic human freedom to govern his own life. In this spirit the caseworker must evaluate the circumstances, to the best of her ability, in which the client's personal welfare, or the community's, justifies her more active participation in the client's affairs.

b. *Authority and law* are realities of organized society. During the last twenty years caseworkers discussed the relationship of the concept of authority with client freedom in practical terms and agreed on their compatibility. Caseworkers were primarily interested in the skills whereby clients could be helped to accept and adjust to the limitations of personal freedom arising from law and authority.

The theory underlying the concepts of law and authority can further clarify that compatibility. The duty of the state, an indispensable institution for social living, is to promote the common good of society and thus to promote the welfare of each member of that society.

Given this duty, the state has a right to the necessary and legitimate means. These means can be summarized as authority and law. Authority is the right of the government to coordinate, regulate, and legislate. Law is the rule or norm of action, determined by authority, according to which individuals and groups are induced to act or are restrained from acting.

Law prevents the individual from abusing or misusing his natural liberty. The use of legitimate authority, for a just and proportionate cause, eventually redounds to the good of the individual.

The experience of caseworkers has been that normally clients are willing to accept and adjust to the limitations set down by authority. Some socially and mentally ill have a neurotic or psychotic aversion to any form of authority, and these need special care.

Others have hostility, not to authority itself, but rather to the authoritative *attitude* of those who administer it. An authoritative attitude is described as a rigid, emotional, domineering manner wherein the person or the administrator of the authority is made to appear as the only basis of the authority. Such an attitude in a social caseworker is inadmissible and unpardonable.

The authoritative *approach,* however, is sometimes necessary and useful in casework, but it must be delicately and skillfully used. The authoritative approach is described as the use of a legitimate, objectively existing civil law or ordinance. In those public agencies where the caseworker is actually or equivalently a public officer, the authoritative approach may be frequent. In private agencies and in public nonauthoritative agencies, the authoritative approach may never have to be used, except as a last resort to prevent an imminent serious danger to the client himself or to other people. The function of using coercive force to compel submission to authority should be avoided by caseworkers and relegated to licensed public servants.

In using the authoritative approach, the spirit, the manner, and the attitude of the caseworker are all-important. The use of authority should be individualized and related to the capacity of the client and to the realities of a given situation.

The caseworker should consider authority as an item in the client's reality situation, and by means of the casework skills and techniques, help the client to accept and adjust to the limitations of his freedom established by authority.

c. *Limitations arising from unwritten standards and norms of the community.* In some closely-knit communities, most often in neighborhoods where one ethnic, racial, or religious group dominates and in small towns or villages, there exist certain opinions, standards, and norms which are not written into any civil law. Such standards may relate to health or to social, moral, or religious personal behavior. These constitute another limitation to client freedom, according to the casework literature.

Since they are unwritten, there is frequently a vagueness and an uncertainty in identifying what these standards are, how they are established, and how they can be accurately recognized.

This obscurity, however, exists primarily on the theoretical level. In the case of a given client, living in a definite community, these unwritten standards may be very clearly defined. Rightly or wrongly they are realities in the client's life.

Caseworkers have not shown much interest in the sociological theories which evaluate the social usefulness of these unwritten standards of the community. The important fact to a caseworker is that these standards are realities in the client's situation. As such, they affect the goals of casework. The client's personal adjustment must include a sound, realistic social adjustment, because as an individual he lives in a social community. Neglect or rejection of the standards and norms of his community will adversely affect his personal adjustment.

Therefore, these standards, which denote limitations to client freedom, are considered by caseworkers nonjudgmentally. Understanding, rather than tolerance or intolerance, is the correct casework attitude. The function of the caseworker is to help the client accept and adjust to them.

d. *Limitations arising from agency function.* Each social agency, whether public or private, has been established to perform a more or less accurately defined function in the community. There is a division of labor among the social agencies, each trying to help the needy members of the community within a limited category.

To achieve its purpose, the social agency has the right and the need to establish limitations to its services. These limitations are incorporated into agency function and concretely expressed in rules, standards, eligibility requirements, and kinds of services offered.

The client has a corresponding duty to respect this right of the agency. If he wishes to use the services of the agency, he is obliged to remain within the framework of the agency's function and to abide by the regulations and requirements of the agency. He has no right to services or assistance which are beyond the scope of the agency's function, or for which he is not eligible. If his application for service is a voluntary one (that is, not required by law), he is free to terminate his contract with the agency which does not offer the service he desires, and seek it elsewhere.

3. *The Role of the Caseworker*. The caseworker is the person who is primarily responsible for applying the principle of client self-determination to practice. The concept of his role in the casework situation, and how he executes it, manifests his attitude to client freedom. The casework literature during the last thirty years had much to say about the caseworker's function specifically as it related to client self-determination. The caseworker's role was stated negatively and positively.

The following activities were considered to be *at variance* with the principle:

a. to assume the principal responsibility for the working out of the problem or need, and allowing the client to play only a subordinate role;

b. to insist on a minute scrutiny of the social or emotional life of client, regardless of the service he requests. A disproportionate diagnosis, as one writer expressed it, reveals the total responsibility and the implied omniscience which the caseworker is assuming. The supposition seems to be that if the caseworker knows all, he can remedy all;

c. to determine the treatment plan and then superimpose it upon the client;

d. to manipulate, directly or indirectly, the social or emotional life of the client. By manipulation is meant the activity of maneuvering the client to assume or change attitudes, to choose or decide upon modes of action in accordance with the caseworker's judgment in such a way that the client is not aware of the process; or if he is aware of it, he feels "moved about" against his will;

e. to persuade. Persuasion is understood to do more than put the client in possession of the facts to make his decision. It means to urge him to accept the caseworker's decision, in such a way as to *weaken* his freedom of choice and decision;

f. to control and direct. This is equivalent to making the choices and decisions, and to allow the client the subordinate role of "participating" or "cooperating"; and

g. to advise and offer plans in such a way that the client feels forced to accept the caseworker's judgment.

The activities of the caseworker which are considered to be *in accord* with client self determination are:

a. to help the client see his problem or need clearly and with perspective. The caseworker's diagnostic study and thinking, his acceptance of the client and identification with him will help the client work through the emotional disturbance which the problem had created and which deprived the client of clarity in seeing himself and his problem;

b. to acquaint the client with the resources in the community and within himself. If there are alternatives, the client is helped to see the significance of each choice. The caseworker may express his own evaluation of each choice and offer suggestions, but in such a way that the client does not feel obliged to accept the caseworker's evaluation and follow his suggestions;

c. to introduce stimuli which will activate the client's own dormant resources. Some specific stimuli are: support, helping to release fears and tensions, information, introduction of new resources, and the stimulus derived from the interaction of two personalities in the casework relationship;

d. to create a nonjudgmental, acceptant relationship environment in which the client can grow and work out his own problems;

e. to help the client move along on his own problem, at his own rate of speed; and

f. to help the client make the choices and decisions that he really wants.

The principle of client self-determination, therefore, does not narrow the scope of the caseworker's activity, except in the area of choices and decisions. It frowns upon the caseworker's "doing things" *for* the client, when the client can do them himself. It discourages "doing things" *to* the client, when he is capable of doing them to himself.

It encourages every other casework activity which can help the client help himself. The caseworker should constantly increase his theoretical knowledge of personality structures which will help to understand each client better. The caseworker should develop skills in observing and evaluating the words, actions, and emotions of the client. In brief, the caseworker should be very active in self-preparation for the role of a helping person, be zealous in the acquisition of the best thinking that is produced in casework and in the allied sciences, and learn to use the best casework skills and techniques.

This ideal concept of the caseworker's function must be coordinated and balanced in some situations, as the casework literature indicates, with the concept of limitations to the client's freedom.

Such was the understanding of the principle of client self-determination in 1950 as it appeared in the American social work literature of the time.

ENDNOTES FOR CHAPTER 4

1 This definition was first proposed in Felix P. Biestek, *The Principle of Client Self-Determination in Social Casework,* (Washington D. C.: The Catholic University of America, 1951) pp. 190-201.

CHAPTER 5

1950—1959

THE KEY to understanding this decade is the concept "democracy." The United States agonized about the means to safeguard democracy as a way of national life, and about the means to defend it from enemies, foreign and domestic. It was an old issue, dating back to the American Revolution, the Bill of Rights, and the Constitution, but it took on new dimensions, painful and dangerous ones.

It was painful because two world wars, the first in 1914-1918 "to make the world safe for democracy" and the second in 1939-1945 to rid the world of totalitarian governments, apparently failed in large part to achieve their purposes.

It was dangerous because a "cold war" existed between the United States and Russia, the two superpowers whose political philosophies were considered to be diametrically opposed. To contain the encroachment of communism, the United States

established the Marshall Plan, the Truman Doctrine, and the
North Atlantic Treaty Organization (NATO). It was a confrontation between the "free world" and the nations behind the "iron
curtain." Democracy and communism were competing for
world leadership.

The decade began with a "police action" in Korea in June
1950, which rapidly developed into a war between the North Koreans, supported by Russia and China, and the South Koreans,
supported principally by the United States. The issue, as seen
by the United States, was to prevent the imposition of communism upon South Korea, ostensibly a democratic nation. The
United States was convinced of the "domino theory"; that is, if
communist nations were successful in absorbing South Korea, a
chain reaction would result, with the possibility of all Asia eventually falling under communist dominion. An armistice was
signed in July 1953, after more than two and a half million people
were killed or wounded.

Nationally, on the home front, concerns were voiced about
the disloyalty of "left wingers" and undercover agents of communism in the entertainment industry and in government jobs.
A few people were accused, and some convicted, of delivering to
Russia secret data concerning atomic fission. The fear of communist infiltration provoked congressional investigations; the
principal one on subversive activities was chaired by Senator
Joseph R. McCarthy of Wisconsin. His anti-Communist
crusade, which began with considerable popular support, soon
was charged with using totalitarian methods in the pursuit of its
purpose. McCarthy was attacked for violations of human rights
in the investigative techniques employed by his subcommittee
and for public accusations without evidence. In 1954 he was
censured by the Senate.

In this decade the nation grew spectacularly in a number of
areas. The population increased to 180 million from 136 million
in 1940. The Gross National Product rose to 500 billion dollars in
1960, more than twice its 1940 size. The unparalleled growth in
industry and commerce stimulated the formation of new super-
corporations. The growth of the cities had been phenomenal;

the United States had rapidly become an urban nation. Nearly half of the population was living in ten great population clusters. The largest of these extended from the borders of Massachusetts and New Hampshire on the north to Washington, D. C. and Virginia on the South. This area included 17 percent of the nation, some thirty-one million people. These growths were mixed blessings; some people interpreted growth to mean prosperity and power; others expressed concern over what was happening to the individual in all of this. For example, William H. Whyte's *The Organization Man*[1] criticized the bureaucracy of big business and the smothering effect it was having upon the individual by its demand for conformity. The concern about individuality was interrelated with the concern about democracy. Was giantism doing the damage that communism was prevented from doing?

An important counter force to giantism's threat to individuality were the steps taken by the civil rights movement at this time. Minorities, especially the black population, developed leadership and methodology in identifying and attacking the violations of their civil rights. The United States Supreme Court in the case of *Brown* v. *The Topeka Board of Education*[2] ruled as unconstitutional the "separate but equal" philosophy as it pertained to education. This led to the challenge of this philosophy in the areas of housing, public facilities, and employment.

In this atmosphere, where concern about democracy and civil rights was an important consideration, the principle of client self-determination felt very much at home. Did the friendliness of the environment contribute to the further development of the principle? And, if so, how? The answer is the task of this chapter.

For the social work profession, this decade had a unique characteristic: it was a period in which the profession, for the first time in its history, was not rushing to meet some national emergency. This was a relatively peaceful period for the profession. Social work had the opportunity for reflection and self-examination, and for putting its house in order.

The accomplishments were notable. They culminated in four principal events: (1) the formation of the National Association of Social Workers (NASW) in 1955; (2) the creation of the Council on Social Work Education (CSWE) in 1952; (3) the publication of a thirteen-volume study of the social work curriculum by the CSWE in 1959; and (4) the promulgation of the NASW Code of Ethics in 1960.

1. *The National Association of Social Workers.*[3] The first objective of this newly created organization was to promote the claim that social work was one profession rather than a collection of several professions. The hope was that practitioners would use, and be known by, one professional title—"social worker," without an adjective indicating setting, such as psychiatric, medical, or school; and without specifying casework, group work, community organization, or research. One title, presumably, would indicate one profession.

The second objective was that this merger would aid in the identification of the generic base of all social work. If social work was one profession, it should be possible to demonstrate that all social workers possess a fundamental body of knowledge and basic competencies essential to the profession. It was considered more important to stress and be known by essential similarities than by differences arising from settings and methods.

The third reason for creating the NASW was the felt need at the time for a single, united voice that could speak for the entire profession to various audiences, such as governmental agencies, the general public, other professions, and the local chapters of social workers. Finally, it was hoped that it would set standards for professional membership and practice, and also serve as an agency for fact-gathering, for public relations, and for promoting publications.

2. *The Council on Social Work Education.* Prior to the establishment of the CSWE in 1952, two organizations competed for the right to set standards and accredit schools of social work. They were the American Association of Schools of Social Work

and the National Association of Schools of Social Administration. The problems and confusion resulting from this situation became intolerable. It took almost six years before full responsibility for professional social work education was contained in one organization, the CSWE. All schools thereafter were governed by the same curriculum policy and the same accrediting standards.

3. *The Thirteen Volume Curriculum Study.* The Hollis-Taylor study[4] revealed in 1951 the varieties and disparities in the policies and practices in social work education at that time. The study identified many serious problems and questions.

When the CSWE was established, it gave top priority to the challenges posed by the Hollis-Taylor study. But instead of taking problem by problem, it decided on an in-depth study of one critical area, namely, the educational objectives. A threefold question was posed: "What are the desirable educational objectives for social work education, into what curriculum areas should they be organized, and what should be their distribution over the undergraduate-graduate continuum?"[5] Most of the recommendations contained in the thirteen volumes were favorably received by social work educators. The one exception was the proposal concerning the undergraduate-graduate continuum, which was rejected by the CSWE membership.

4. *The NASW Code of Ethics.* In October 1960 the Delegate Assembly of the NASW adopted a code of ethics, a brief, two-page statement which consisted of a preamble and fourteen propositions. The principal motivation for adopting this code seemed to be the striving for professionhood; that is, since one of the essential requirements of a profession was a code of ethics, and since social work wanted to be recognized as a bona fide profession, it had to have one. The quality of the code seemed to be of less importance than its existence. It has been criticized by social workers from the day it was adopted as being an inadequate instrument for promoting ethical behavior among its members. Its survival may be a disproof of the criticisms, or it may be indicative of the profession's disinterest in the subject. Its historical significance is that social work thereby

met the final technical qualification of membership among the professions.

THEORY

The theory of client self-determination as it was understood at the end of the previous decade was briefly summarized in the previous chapter. Was anything really new added to the theory in the 1950-1959 decade? Yes and no. No, in the sense that there were no substantive reversals in the theory, no spectacular occurrences, no violent debates, and no utterly new discoveries. Yes, in the sense of an evolutionary growth and development wherein the ideas of previous decades were tested, confirmed, and enriched.

1. *Democracy and Social Work.* To appropriately appreciate the results of this evolutionary process, it may be profitable to recall the nation's preoccupation with democracy. It is the framework within which the development of the principle occurred.

The agony suffered by the nation concerning democracy as a form of government and as a way of life influenced, predictably, the thoughts and concerns of social work.

> The profession of social work, like all professions, is an occupational subculture imbedded in the matrix of the larger culture. The dominant ideas and moods of the enveloping culture exert a subtle, but inexorable influence on the ideas and moods that social workers, as social workers, regard as right and proper.[6]

The social work profession, as seen in the literature of this decade, accepted and identified itself with democracy. Benjamin Youngdahl voiced a common conviction of social workers when he said: "We have implicit faith in democracy and in democratic institutions . . . ."[7] In its preamble, the NASW Code of Ethics stated: "Professional social work is based on humanitarian, democratic ideals," and as far as is known, no criticism or challenge has ever been voiced against this statement.[8] Donald Howard added an interesting dimension to the relationship between social work and democracy by calling social work "a creature of democracy."[9]

In discussing the education of professional social workers, Arlien Johnson observed that the origin of modern social work in the United States drew upon the basic democratic philosophy as found in the humanitarian and religious movements of the 19th century. She noted that "liberty, equality, and fraternity" have found their expression in American democracy and have become the cornerstone of social work philosophy.[10] They are found in such values as the dignity and worth of the individual, his right to freedom of choice and action, and the importance of group effort and majority rule.

In the context of the national scene, the desire of social work to express its identification with democracy should be no surprise. It was a very popular thing to do. But what was surprising was the fervor with which this was said. Even a cursory scan of the lead articles in *The Social Welfare Forum* during these ten years demonstrates the emotional flavor. Why the fervor?

The first and most fundamental reason probably was that social work sincerely and completely agreed with democracy's philosophy of man and of human relationships. "Democracy . . . as a way of life is a system of ethical concepts which must pervade the totality of human relationships, be they political, economic, social or spiritual."[11] What happened was something like this, figuratively: social work glanced over the walls of its self-made ghetto one day and saw in the outside world a respect and even a reverence for something it itself treasured, namely, freedom and self-determination. Associated with this was social work's conviction that it had much to contribute to promoting democracy.

> Social work, at least as it is known in the United States, is both a creature of democracy and one of the creators of a more thorough-going democracy. Civil liberty, an inescapable concomitant of democracy, not only undergirds social work as we know it, but in turn is enhanced by social work.[12]

Social work felt that it was a product, a creature, a result of democracy, and as such it benefited from the broader framework of democratic principles and ideals. It also felt that it contributed to democracy by providing a democratic experience to people whose right to freedom of choice frequently was in jeopardy. The principle of client self-determination gave direction to the social services offered to a segment of society which often was neglected by society.

Another reason for the fervor, perhaps a somewhat unconscious one, was social work's bid for acceptance by the society of that day. Social workers were still licking their wounds from the criticisms that they "pushed people around" and that they were incapable of really helping people. By identifying with the nation's concern about democracy, social work now had the opportunity to improve its public image and reverse some of the criticisms hurled at it in previous decades.

As social workers continued to study the mutuality in the relationship between democracy and social work, they recalled that both claimed to have the same supreme value, namely, the worth and dignity of the human person.

Many statements about the value of the human person were found in the social work literature of this decade. The CSWE curriculum study identified it as the first among the "highly abstract values."

> Each human being should be regarded by all others as an object of infinite worth. He should be preserved in a state commensurate with his innate dignity and protected from suffering.[13]

The preamble to the NASW Code of Ethics contained this paragraph:

> Social work practice is a public trust that requires of its practitioners integrity, compassion, faith in the dignity and worth of human beings, respect for individual differences, a commitment to service, and a dedication to truth.[14]

Social workers unanimously agreed on this value. There might have been differences on how it was verbalized and there certainly were differences on how it was to be implemented. But, stated in abstract terms, it had universal approval.

The social work profession felt that it had paid a penalty for championing this value throughout history. It had been called all kinds of nasty names because it fought for the welfare of the "social failures." Social workers were often made to feel like a radical minority that was causing social unrest by catering to social misfits who were demanding more and more from society and doing less and less for themselves.

Now, in this decade, social work heard democracy proclaiming this same fundamental value. It was contained, of course, in the Bill of Rights and other foundation statements of the United States. But it was freshly reiterated at this time because of the felt dangers to democracy. So it was nothing really new. But it had a new meaning for social work. The feeling of being a pesty minority was softened. Social work started to feel that it "belonged." Being a social worker became a little more "respectable."

Social work, however, was not naive on this point. It knew that human value and dignity were sometimes violated, perhaps often—at times legally—by democratic institutions. This was something social work was eventually going to have to fight against in a more deliberate and organized manner—perhaps in a later decade. But for now, a little friendship was better than none at all. An agreement on some theoretical basics was better than constant animosity. At that time it was good news indeed that, whatever their differences might be, the social work profession and a democratic society concurred on the supreme value.

The logical sequence of concepts, from democracy—to worth and dignity of the person—to self-determination, was stated by Friedlander:

> The feelings, attitudes, orientation, and practice of social workers in the American culture are inspired by the following democratic values: conviction of the inherent worth, the integrity, and the

dignity of the individual. . . . The second generic principle is the
conviction that the individual, who is in economic, personal, or
social need has the right to determine himself what his needs are
and how they should be met.[15]

2. *Definitions of the Principle*. It was in this decade that the
principle of client self-determination was explicitly defined for
the first time, and when articles and books dealing with the
principle *ex professo* first appeared.[16] The definitions did not
substantively vary among themselves, but each had its own
emphasis and style. One of the first to appear was Helen
Perlman's. It emphasized self-determination as an inalienable
limited right.

> Now it becomes necessary to reexamine what we mean by self-
> determination. We affirm again that to determine what one wants
> to do, to live by the exercise of one's own will rather than by the
> will of another—these are the inalienable rights of free men . . .
> limited rights . . . because in order that they be exercised by all,
> they must be bounded by certain responsibilities of each indi-
> vidual to others and to the common will of the community or
> expressed in custom and law . . . our rights to self-determination
> are limited in many ways . . . by explicit or implicit expecta-
> tions of us, by custom, by fashion, by ingrained habit. Full
> self-determination is an illusion. . . .[17]

Bowers put self-determination into a broader context, defining it as a necessary means to achieving life's goals. He also
pointed to the limitations of personal freedom.

> (Self-determination) . . . is the principle that the human being can
> attain his own perfection only through the exercise of his free will,
> that he has both the right and the need to be free in his choices. To
> each person has been given the responsibility of living his life in
> such a manner as to achieve its goals, immediate goals as well as
> the ultimate goals. . . . This freedom is limited only by the restric-
> tions of law, both natural and positive, and in situations in which
> there exists some incapacity of the individual to use his freedom in
> an advantageous way. Occasionally, we have the obligation to
> prevent a person from misusing or abusing his freedom, but we
> should always assume that he is capable of making his own

constructive decisions, unless there is clear evidence to the contrary.[18]

The next definition included the right and the need of the client to freedom and the limitations of that right. And it added a reference to the social worker's function in implementing the principle.

> The principle of client self-determination is the practical recognition of the right and need of clients to freedom in making their own choices and decisions in the casework process. Caseworkers have a corresponding duty to respect that right, recognize that need, stimulate and help to activate that potential for self-direction by helping the client to see and use the available and appropriate resources of the community and of his own personality. The client's right to self-determination, however, is limited by the client's capacity for positive and constructive decision-making, by the framework of civil and moral law, and by the function of the agency.[19]

Henry Maas preferred to divide the subject into two parts: "the principle of participation" and "the principle of self-determination"; the latter he called the "important corollary" of the former. He stressed these two principles as guides to the caseworker's role and function.[20] Friedlander, Bisno, and Gordon Hamilton made statements in their books about client self-determination that could be considered partial definitions, but these added little to what had been written by others.[21]

a. *Concerning the right* of the client to self-determination. A variety of bases for the right were offered: it flowed as a necessary consequence of man's worth and dignity; because man had the responsibility for pursuing life's goals, he had the right to freely choose the appropriate means to those goals.[22] Discussion of the right to freedom was minimal, perhaps because there was no challenge to it, at least on a theoretical level, in American society of the time. It was a conviction on which there seemed to be universal agreement. Where there were differences, they seemed to be due to the styles of expression rather than to thought content. The following excerpt is not untypical.

As I understand it, the democratic philosophy implies those basic tenets which are the core of our social and political life, and which embrace a common creed—freedom, equality, and the pursuit of happiness—grounded in the primacy of the dignity of man and supremacy of the human spirit.[23]

b. *Concerning the need* of the client for self-determination. Earlier, when social workers wrote of the need of the client for self-determination, they gave the impression that they made a new discovery or were expressing a daring idea. There was a tentativeness in the statements, as if they were waiting for experience or empirical research to test and confirm it. In this decade the hesitation was gone, and the need for freedom was stated as if it were a venerable truism. Self-determination was needed for the client's personality growth and maturity, emotional adjustment in times of stress, confidence in self as he finds solutions for his problems, and avoidance of unhealthy dependence upon others. Friedlander's statement is probably a typical expression.

The caseworker guides him to his own acceptance of his problems and to his own decision to find a new way. His freedom of choice forestalls any frustrated, discouraged feeling that he is asking for help, that another person is interfering with his private life or managing his affairs. He regains confidence in himself when he recognizes his ability to find solutions for his problems and to decide on his way of following through.[24]

c. *Concerning limitations* to client self-determination. By 1950 social workers generally were agreed that the client's right to self-determination, as all other human rights, is subject to limitations because no right is absolute. The limitations were identified as arising from the client's capacity, law, agency function, and the standards and norms of the community. In the 1950-1959 decade the discussions of these limitations continued and a few others were added.

The discussion of the first limitation (arising from the client's capacity) attempted to apply the idea to the realities of life. Ideally, all persons should have equal opportunities and resources for self-determination. In reality, however, individuals differ and are not really equal, due to differences in physical, social, intellectual, and emotional inheritance, conditions, and events.

> The ideal of each client being fully self-determined is modified by the realities in each individual instance. Since the capacity to make decisions varies from client to client, the worker is aware of the client's mental and physical capacity to act for himself and does not force him to greater self-determination than he has capacity for. . . . The capacity of clients has degrees.[25]

Perlman indicated that emotional stress and anxiety distort perception and consequently diminish a person's capacity for self-determination.

> Self-determination is limited for all of us at those times when emotional stress or involvement is so great that our perception of what is realistic is dimmed, our understanding is dulled, or our perspective is distorted. At such times our capacity to be self-determining with judgment and objectivity is obviously impaired.[26]

Perlman identified another cause of incapacity: inadequate awareness or knowledge of the consequences of a decision. To act with freedom, the person should understand the actual or potential results that will follow from his decision.

> True self-determination can only take place when we know the results or the meaning of the choice of action that we make. When an individual is not equipped by knowledge or clear understanding to judge what the consequences or implications of his choice will be, he is not free to choose. At such a time his choice may have to be to trust or not to trust what is accepted to be the responsible and more expert opinion of someone else.[27]

Customary procedures and habits are another category of limitations that affect the person's capacity for self-determination, according to Perlman. These limitations, however, absolve the person from the tyranny of endless little decisions and free him for significant problem-solving tasks.

Our rights to self-determination are limited in many subtle ways of which we are not even conscious—by explicit or implicit expectations of us, by custom, by fashion, by ingrained habit. . . . Actually, limits are necessary to our integrity and even to our survival. Our lives would be intolerable if we had to make a decision about each action we had to take. Our physical and mental energies would be totally dissipated, and we would be so busy exercising self-determination that there would be no possibility of focusing our thought and energy on new and major problems of living.[28]

In regard to law and civil authority as a limitation to self-determination, social workers during this decade strove to see the positive uses of authority and law. By and large, they viewed law as an essential reality for the functioning of society, and considered authority as a potentially constructive influence in the lives of people. Social workers continued to distinguish between legitimate and illegitimate authority, between legitimate authority and an authoritative attitude. They continued to develop skills to help clients accept and adjust to limitations arising from law. Studt and Mencher discussed the differences between authority and power.[29] This distinction had more meaning for social action as an interventive method than for the principle of client self-determination.

There was an awareness of the misuses of law and of the injustices inherent in some social structures created by law. But social workers at this time were notably quiet about these abuses. Why? One of the reasons was the profession's identification with "democracy" discussed earlier in this chapter. Another reason was the general tone and predominant attitude of American society at the time; social work as a subculture partook of this quiescent attitude. This decade was the lull before the storm. In the 1960s the respect for law, authority, and order would diminish to a significant degree. The focus would be on the injustices that authority was protecting, on social action, and on changing the unjust structures and institutions of society. That, however, was still to come.

The limitation to client freedom arising from agency function continued to be recognized: the agency had a right and a need to specify and delimit its function and service; the client did not have a right to demand services beyond that specification. However, some criticism was addressed to two conditions, associated with agency function, that adversely affected the self-determination of clients.

The first was the "undue emphasis upon the reduction of caseloads." This happened principally in public assistance agencies. The constant cry of some social workers in these agencies for years had been the deleterious effect of large caseloads on social workers and on clients. The charge was that social workers simply did not have the time to do a quality job and hence were severely criticized as second-rate professionals. At the same time the clients were cheated of services that were written into agency manuals but were not implemented because the social workers lacked the necessary time due to overloading. In some instances, clients paid the price of the rebellion of social workers against overloading. The following excerpt voiced the concern of many social workers regarding this problem.

> Undue emphasis upon the reduction of caseloads . . . has been shown by experience to lead to an unimaginative and insensitive approach to recipient's needs and often to most restrictive, punitive practices which have destroyed self-respect and created additional dependency, thus defeating even their stated objectives.[30]

The second criticism was directed at "bureaucratic red tape." Some agencies, like some persons, prematurely develop a case of hardened arteries. Their definition of agency function and services, originally made with full justification and legitimation, hardened into an inflexibility that amounted to a refusal of services to people fully entitled to them. This "red tape" in some agencies was an unjust limitation of client freedom. Typical of the comments on this problem is the following.

> Before it is too late, a "breakthrough" of the bureaucracy of social work must be made to a vast public. People are so irritated by what they call "red tape" and by what seems to be a cold, technical approach that they turn to the black market in adoptions, the

unsupervised home for the aging, or they stay in the dark places of poverty and distress rather than seek help.[31]

d. *Concerning the role of the social worker* in implementing the principle. At the end of the previous decade, the obligation of the social worker to help the client exercise his right to self-determination was clearly recognized. The literature specified, as summarized in Chapter 4, the activities of the social worker in diagnosis and treatment that were in accord with the principle and those that were at variance with it.

To fulfill this obligation, it was stressed, the social worker needed knowledge of personality structures, skills in observing and evaluating words, actions, and emotions of the individual. The source of this knowledge, in large part, was psychiatry. It provided much of the knowledge concerning human development and behavior that guided social work practice.

3. *New Factors Influencing the Principle.* A number of additional factors in the 1950-1959 decade influenced the theory of client self-determination. They were: (a) the rediscovery of the role of culture; (b) ego psychology; (c) the multiproblem and nonvoluntary client; (d) the "problem-solving" casework model; (e) clients with character disorders; and (f) short-term casework. A brief discussion of each of these factors as they affected the self-determination principle is presented in the following paragraphs.

a. *The concept of culture.* In the 1950-1959 decade, rather suddenly and very belatedly, the "social " in social work was rediscovered, and concomitantly, cultural anthropology and other social sciences. Why these sciences were neglected by social work for so long a time is a mystery about which historians might speculate. The knowledge areas that appeared immediately relevant to social work revolved around the concepts of culture and values. Almost overnight social workers spoke of the social perspectives of behavior as a new source of knowledge. Articles appeared which focused directly upon the nature of culture and the cultural processes and on the impact of culture in shaping and molding the multidimensional demands made upon each individual as a part of the subgroups and subcultures to which he belonged.[32]

> Clearly, if the worker is really to understand his client, he must be sensitive to the impact that his client's cultural values have upon the meanings he attaches to the world about him.[33]

The following quotation is typical. It relates culture and value to treatment goals and self-determination.

> In setting goals for treatment, the worker should endeavor to evaluate the appropriateness of his value-laden concepts of desirable behavior and adequate social functioning. If the worker makes the error of considering his own values "universals," his treatment efforts are not likely to succeed. The worker should endeavor to understand the client's values, recognizing that relatively few standards can be validly applied to all members of society. Failure to recognize relative personal and cultural patterns, in fact, can only defeat the purpose of helping persons to attain self-fulfillment in a democratic sense.[34]

b. *Ego psychology*. Building further upon the social perspectives of behavior was the interest given to ego psychology by social workers. Ego psychology provided an alternative framework for understanding individual behavior. Some social workers charged that Freud's psychoanalytic theories, the predominant model for psychiatric casework, portrayed persons as being controlled by internal psychic forces and impulses and by behavior patterns molded in early childhood quite difficult to change. In contrast, ego psychology offered a more optimistic approach to man by focusing upon the inherent resources within the individual and the environment. The capacity of the ego to promote positive change, to enhance the social environment for achieving, learning and building social relationships was here emphasized.[35]

Within this model, the client manages himself more constructively through modifying his "destructive defenses" and expanding his own resourcefulness. Ego psychology viewed man, not as the "controlled one" but as the "controller." In this light then, the worker's role was to further the client's motivating power within himself and to "strengthen his command over his own destiny" by helping him to tap this "unused capacity to change" found within himself.[36]

c. *The multiproblem and nonvoluntary clients*. As the implications of ego psychology continued to be explored it seemed to follow that some reconsideration had to be made of those clients for whom the "more traditional" approaches of social services seemed ineffective or inappropriate, especially those who had been categorized as "multiproblem," "nonvoluntary," or "hopeless." In the process of reevaluation some significant factors emerged which seemed to explain resistance or rejection of service. These included the client's mistrust of the worker's intentions, the degree to which the client participated in the decision to seek help, and the client's feelings of helplessness and hopelessness in responding to the problem situation.[37]

The clients were often angry and rejected society's standards and authority because they felt overwhelmed. Consequently they came across as nonconforming, aggressive, neglected, and deprived[38] and were labeled as being controlled by events.[39] Further examination revealed other factors that needed to be considered, such as communcation barriers between client and worker due to differences in social class, race, or ethnic backgrounds. In some instances, what appeared as the rejection of service was in fact the presence of a communication lag between the two. From the client's point of view, to accept help implied an admission of failure, failure to be his own master and failure to adequately fulfill his social roles.[40]

To counter this, the caseworker had to build a relationship which would offset these feelings of isolation and alienation. By projecting acceptance and sincerity, the worker had to reach out to the client and foster feelings of trust. "Reaching out" was not simply an act or technique but rather a "frame of mind, a psychological readiness, a determination of the social worker to find a way to help the patient."[41]

By reaching out, the worker is able to provide direction and support for the client without violating the principle of self-determination. The worker can be "giving" without being demanding or coercive. By clarifying the nature of the services available, the goals of the relationship, the possible alternatives, and the client's own dormant resources, the client is reassured that the ultimate decision is his. This may lead the client and the worker to a stronger casework relationship, and the client to "greater individual happiness and growth."[42]

d. *The problem-solving model.* During this period another casework model was introduced, called "problem-solving." This built conceptually on the Diagnostic and Functional models and on insights drawn from ego psychology. As a synthesis, it viewed the individual's inability to cope with a problem as due to some lack of motivation, capacity, or opportunity to work on, solve, or mitigate the problem in an appropriate way.[43] The goal was to assist the client to become more effective in managing his present problems. To this end, the worker sought to utilize the "effectance drive" of the client. This drive was defined as the "innate push within man to extend himself, to use his powers in order to be an active cause of happenings, to seek pleasure not merely to release tension but in new experiences that use and reward his competence."[44]

To achieve this, the worker's activity encompassed:

- releasing, energizing, and giving direction to the client's motivation;
- releasing and helping to exercise the client's mental, emotional, and action capacities for coping with his problems; and
- finding or creating opportunities for the client to utilize in working out his problem.[45]

This compelled the caseworker to see the client as a unique individual, to understand individual patterns or variations of behavior and resources. It also stressed three basic elements: the client's volition (what he wants, what he wants to cast out of his life or to make part of his life), the client's capacity (what he is able to do about what he wants), and the client's opportunities (what is actually available to him).[46]

e. *Clients with character disorders*. As these new aspects of casework theory continued to develop, the profession found itself struggling with another group of clients who were characterized as impulse ridden, very demanding, and quite difficult to work with within the traditional methods of social casework. These were clients with character disorders.

Ego psychology believed that all clients have the ability to be self-determining, even the very sick and those with character disturbances. The challenge here is to help the client see that he has the capacity to change, and that he must use it if he is to be helped to increase this social functioning. The situation is further complicated by the equalizing role which the worker has to maintain, balancing on the one hand teaching these clients how to take greater responsibility for their actions, while on the other hand, avoiding making demands upon them which are "too heavy for their capacities" or creating "stress" and "frustration" which might "perpetuate or exacerbate" their problems.[47]

The worker's task is to help the client incorporate proper social norms and develop an improved ego structure in order to function successfully in society. Several suggestions were proposed as appropriate alternatives in these situations:

- to help the client, through identification, to modify his ego-ideal to conform with more successful individuals;
- to help the client substitute ego models with which he can easily identify; and
- to help him substitute membership and reference groups which are in harmony with the standards of the majority of the community.[48]

To do this effectively, however, the worker was put into a position of having to actively use his authority, especially in the setting of limits for the client. This raised questions about the viability of client self-determination in these instances. The response was that in working with clients categorized as having character disorders, it is crucial that the client be helped to do for himself.

The goal of casework, in whatever setting, is to enable the client to do and act for himself. . . . Casework can help (these) individuals to perform their social roles with ease and spontaneity, with satisfaction to themselves and to others who are in interpersonal interaction with them, and thus to function better in their social world.[49]

f. *Short-term casework*. One further development in social casework requires consideration at this point: short-term service. Short-term service was used more deliberately and planfully in this decade than ever before. Why, and what does this have to do with self-determination? In response to the why, agencies found themselves with too many clients—and long waiting lists increased the stress of the clients. Some agencies invoked a conviction of the Functional school that the use of time limitations could be a valid part of the treatment plan.

To the second question, there was not an easy reply. If time is being limited by choice or by necessity, how much of it can be given to self-determination? By limiting time, you also structure the role of the caseworker by making it almost necessary for him to be more aggressive in order to achieve the desired goals. As noted before and rooted in the same questions of control, the worker is more active and it appears as if results are more important than process. Because of the time limitations, certain sacrifices of process seem necessary. With short-term service, more direct recommendations, worker aggressiveness, and manipulation seemed inevitable.

The debate was never really resolved. To some, the sacrifice of process to worker authority and manipulation seemed a reversion to the old time manipulation of the 1920s and 1930s, a potentially dangerous trend. To others, the authoritative role of the worker was justified on the grounds that it was still the client who was asking for a service and in the end, it was still the client's right "to make a negative as well as positive decision."[50]

PRACTICE

Thus far in this historical study, emphasis has been placed upon self-determination in the casework method. Casework was where the principle was discussed and debated to a far greater extent than in any other social work method. Group work and community organization borrowed extensively the results of casework's struggle with client self-determination and appropriately applied them to groups and communities. But they were not just borrowers. They introduced the new concept of representativeness, which will be subsequently discussed at greater length. They also served as a bridge between this decade and the next one. In this decade there was still a belief that if people were freed and strengthened, they could manage their environment. In the 1960-1969 decade that belief gave way to an opposite conviction that the environment was replete with unjust social structures, that real self-determination could not be practiced within those structures, that intervention at the societal level was necessary, and that social work needed to retool for social action and social policy planning.

The following very brief references to the principle of client self-determination in group work and community organization are intended merely to illustrate two observations: (a) how fundamental and how undisputed the principle is considered by these two methods; and (b) how they served as a bridge to the social action emphasis of the succeeding decade.

1. *Group Work.* The basic reference defining group work was found in the position adopted by the American Association of Group Workers.

> Through his participation the group worker aims to affect the group process so that decisions come about as a result of knowledge and a sharing and integration of ideas, experiences, and knowledge rather than as a result of domination from within or without the group. Through experience he aims to produce these relations with other groups and the wider community which contribute to responsible citizenship, mutual understanding between cultural, religious, economic or social groupings in the community and a participation in the constant improvement of our society toward democratic goals.[51]

Here was emphasized the shared decision-making process and exchange of ideas between worker and group members within a democratic frame of reference or philosophical value milieu. Group work helps to develop the individual's capacities for adequate social functioning in a democratic society, for opportunities for self-expression, and for development of self-respect and respect for others through "ways of working together that are associated with the term democracy."[52]

The American Association of Group Workers noted that the leadership in the group setting rested upon the common assumptions of a democratic society, namely:

- the opportunity for each individual to fulfill his capacity in freedom;
- to respect and appreciate others; and
- to assume his social responsibility in maintaining and constantly improving the democratic society.[53]

This, in turn, established the foundation for the principles of social group work. As summarized by Konopka, they included:

a. the right of the individual and the group to self-determination as long as this right is not misused by limiting that of others;

b. the right of individuals and groups to participation in decision-making;

c. the ethical use of confidential material by the social worker;

d. the use of the group work method only when competent judgment calls for its value to the group; and

e. the use of consultation when need arises.[54]

The group worker then is viewed as a combination of social scientist, practitioner, and philosopher, blending values and beliefs with professional knowledge and methods. The worker enables the group members, individually and collectively, to achieve greater independence and increased feelings of self-worth while at the same time recognizing the mutual interdependence of people.[55] By helping group members to develop their own unique personalities through the exercise of freedom of choice, she brings the group to the point of viewing the development of values as a shared, social process. The success of the group work method is closely related to the demonstration of client self-determination within the group.

2. *Community Organization.* In the community organization method of social work in this period, a major development occurred relative to client self-determination: this was the principle of representativeness. Until this decade, community organization appeared to be a broad, sometimes all-inclusive term used to describe a range of community based activities and services. There was considerable discussion as to whether community organization referred to a method, a process, a series of activities, the structure of an organization, or a particular point of view.[56]

In the 1957 *Social Work Yearbook*, a synthesis definition of community organization was proposed which encompassed community organization as a process, a field of activity, a geographic area and/or a community interest.

> Community organization is a process used by professional workers engaged in health and welfare planning. It consists, in part, of the skillful use of "enabling" techniques through which social workers engaged in community organization practice make it possible by providing in direct leadership, for citizen groups to work out problems involved in coordinating the complex range of social services now found in most communities, and to modify and change services in the light of new ones. Implicit in this activity is the use of a professional approach to the problems of identifying areas of social need and of promoting and interpreting programs that will meet them. Community organization is also a field of activity in social work and as such is occupied by agencies whose primary function is social planning, coordination, interpretation, or the joint financing of direct service agencies.[57]

The problem for the professional then was to define community organization in such a way as to make it practical and functional. Hendry observed that in community organization, a true sense of partnership between the people and the specialist-professional had to exist, otherwise collective goals could not be attained. "People support what they have a share in creating and people share when it is acknowledged that they have a stake in the situation involved."[58]

Community organization, restated in a positive relationship with the common base of social work, embodies the generic principles of:

- helping the individual, the group, or the community to help himself or itself;
- beginning where the group, individual, or community is and moving at a meaningful pace;
- focusing upon the individual, the group, or the community as well as on the problem; and
- taking into account the stage of development of the individual, the group, or the community.[59]

A number of practices in community organization attempted to implement client self-determination, such as developing "citizen participation," "citizen input," and "citizen representatives." One area of particular significance was the concept of representativeness.

Until this time problems related to representativeness delt with definitions. That is, some contended representativeness was the identified *role* which an individual carried from one group to another. Others contended it referred to the structure utilized in intergroup process to create a group consisting of individuals who "represent or are representative of groups in the community."[60] Still others distinguished among representation as the delegation of authority which clearly defined role responsibilities, the nondelegate representative who "lacks the authority to act on behalf of the constituency, but has the ability to influence it," and the representative from an unorganized group who lacks the authority but who speaks as a symbol of the group, for example an aged person, a physician, a black.[61]

Critical to this discussion was the principle "the consent of the governed."[62]   This assumed new meaning as the Housing Act of 1954 extended client self-determination from a concept based soley upon either ethical principles or moral law to a concept now supported by civil law. Point Seven of the Workable Program for Urban Renewal of this Act required that

> . . . any political entity which wishes to participate in federally aided programs for the renewal of blighted areas of a city must provide in its planning for community-wide participation on the part of individuals and representative citizen organizations which will help to provide both in the community generally and in selected areas the understanding and support which is necessary to insure success.[63]

This requirement of evidence of citizen participation served to stimulate many to demand participation as their legitimate, legal right. It also fostered the growth of many welfare rights organizations and increased awareness in the issues of community control.

Many refused to honor or accept representativeness, even as a legal construct. Concern was voiced that it could become a tool of the power structure and be diverted from its intended purposes. Some argued that true representativeness could never be realized in situations where the needs of the "common good" held priority over the rights and needs of the individual. Nevertheless, by becoming a legal precedent through federal regulations, citizen participation in the decision-making process was required. This was new. This was different. It now fell to many social workers to discharge their responsibilities by fostering client self-determination at the community level.

> Our responsibility, and our obligation, is to the entire community, as it is to the whole person and to the whole group in casework and social group work practice. That responsibility must be expressed . . . by creating the climate and helping to set the stage wherein and whereon individuals and groups may be free and encouraged to determine community needs, establish priorities, select their own solutions, and jointly decide upon and then pursue a common plan of action.[64]

3. *Settings*. As was true in the previous decades, much of the discussion relative to client self-determination centered upon

practical problems of implementation. Special attention was given those clients for whom self-determination seemed doubtful, less relevant, or impractical. Specifically included were the aged, the mentally ill, the mentally retarded, children, clients in correction settings, and those receiving public assistance.

One frequent flaw which seemed to underscore the questioning of relevance was found in stereotyping these groups of clients. For instance, the social worker needed to deal with the stereotype which portrayed the aged client as a doddering, senile individual, unable to reason or make sound judgments for himself. Likewise, the levels or degrees of mental retardation needed to be understood in order to offset the caricature of the retarded as imbecilic or moronic.

To counter this, the need to individualize clients, to recognize the unique strengths and limitations of each individual, and to build into the casework relationship opportunities for the client to develop his personal resources underscored the discussion related to client self-determination. Regardless of the type of limitation or handicap, the worker was responsible for assessing each client's capacity to plan for himself.

Perhaps the danger of severe damage being done to the client's self-respect and self-esteem is even greater if self-determination is disregarded. These clients may be affected more because of their heightened sensitivity and vulnerability based on their prior experiences. The consequences of failing to assure self-determination are the same for all clients: increased incidence of depression, feelings of rejection, regressive behavior, and most important, feelings of devaluation as a person of dignity and worth.

For those who worked with clients at either end of the life span, the young or the aged, similiar concerns were present and likewise, parallel cautions were expressed. Because the young and the aged seemed to be impulsive, illogical, incapable of rational thinking, or too emotional and immature, this was not to be considered sufficient grounds for denying them their right of self-determination. Each child and each aged client has the same need to be self-determining, to be in situations which would enable him to maximize his strengths and resources. To paraphrase one writer, age, in and of itself, is not a disability that prevents younger or older persons from expressing their own ideas and making their own decisions.[65]

The child's involvement in the decision-making process was considered to be a critical preparation for adulthood and maturity. All too frequently children were "seen but not heard"; consequently, the adults in the child's world failed to communicate with him or understand him and his needs. For the child, the consequences were far more serious because he also had lost the opportunity for a beneficial, meaningful relationship with an adult.

For the mentally ill or retarded client, self-determination was considered a valuable element in the casework relationship. Although these clients might have vastly different problems, their basic self-needs remained the same as with all people.

The only difference (and that too can be debated) is the need for more careful case planning and management by the worker. This required sound assessment and understanding of the client's strengths and limitations. The worker should encourage the client to participate at the upper levels of his abilities and social functioning, thus enabling the client to create a sense of identity and achievement by building his perception of personal worth.

Specific concern was expressed for the institutionalized patient and the often negative effect which the institution had upon the client. Especially noted were those factors which appeared to condition the client and cause him to shape his behavior to meet the needs of the institution rather than his own perceived needs. The findings as reported by Goffman in his book *Asylums*[66], or life as depicted by Kesey in *One Flew Over the Cuckoo's Nest*, [67] supported the contention that there was much within the institutionalized role of the patient which was not in the service of developing self-confidence, his ability to live a self-determining life, or even in his recovery.

The caseworker was challenged to seek out or even create opportunities which would counteract the negatives of

institutionalization. To do this, he needed to have an awareness of the climate of the dominant culture and subcultures of
the institution, and in particular, to view peer group pressure
as a reality to be understood.

For another client population, children or adults under court
supervision, self-determination was viewed as doubtful by some
social workers. This was due in part to the role of the worker as
agent of the court, an authority figure. This placed the burden of
responsibility upon the worker to demonstrate positive, constructive use of this authority. The worker was urged to be an
enabler, helping the client to function with as great a degree of
freedom as possible, and influencing the institution "to orient its
program to function effectively for an individual."[68]

The social worker in corrections was faced with major tasks:
to understand the philosophy and the orientation of the institutional administration and to make its services beneficial for the
client. The first task was difficult because of the philosophical
dichotomy of correctional institutions. On the one side, the
institution was "to hold the sentenced person in custody" while
at the same time it was also expected to reform him.[69] If the
administrative focus was on being punitive, the role of the
worker would have to involve interpreting authority and helping
the inmate to become reconciled to the demands of society and
of the institution as the representative of that society. The social
worker must decide whether his identification lies with authority or with the client and what his role is in relation to punishment, deprivation, or whatever the forms of discipline might be
labeled. If, however, the aim of the institution is on rehabilitation and "reforming" the client, the authority role could be
offset by the "therapeutic" role.[70] For the corrections worker,
this dilemma was not easily resolved nor was it a responsibility
that could be evaded, as Elliott Studt noted.

> The student reads: "Do not impose your will and purposes upon
> the client. Leave him free to choose his own direction." He has
> heard that to help he should be non-directive. He wonders how he
> can use these and still function as a probation officer. . . . The
> solution for his problem is twofold. In the first place, he must be-

come comfortable within himself about authority and this requires an inner reliance from the leftover battles of adolescence and a new awareness of the role of authority in human development. After clarification of this feeling, he needs to define precisely the responsibilities he must carry by reason of his function.[71]

Authority, used as a constructive force, can be a stabilizing element in the life of an individual. When used wisely and discriminately, it may be a consistent source of strength upon which the individual can draw. The caseworker must establish a balance between the authority implicit in his role and his professional commitment to respecting the client's right and need for self-determination. As one worker put it:

> You can't be dictatorial in any way, shape or fashion. You can't impose your own point of view on them (clients). They are individuals with their own ways of life. You have to accept them as human beings with problems just like you have. The hardest thing is to convince him that the choice is his—that you're not trying to force him to be something he doesn't want to be.[72]

One group of clients remains to be discussed—the public assistance client. As had been the case in the earlier decades, this group of clients, especially the Aid to Dependent Children recipient, provoked intense, frequently deeply biased and prejudicial debate. One wonders why it continues to come up, time and again. What intensified the concerns during this decade was the clarification of the rights of the client and the legal demands he or she could make upon the system as part of those rights. With the passage of the 1956 Amendments to the Social Security Act, significant impetus was given to the *social* purposes of public assistance programs. Services beyond the mere rendering of monetary allocations were stressed. These services would:

    a. build upon a philosophy of administration that requires respect for the persons to whom assistance is given;

    b. offer diverse services of both a preventive and protective nature to assist the client in returning to self-dependency and self-support or will be a means of sustaining a wholesome way of living for the child and his family. This embodies the notion of maintaining and strengthening the home;[73]

c. assist people in living useful, purposeful lives consistent with their innate dignity and individual potentialities.[74]

This was further identified as a turning point in public assistance when the Bureau of Public Assistance and the American Welfare Association issued a joint statement on the philosophy of American public welfare.

a. All people should have the opportunity to secure the basic needs for living. When they cannot meet these needs, it is the responsibility of government to assist in meeting them through appropriate sources.

b. Everyone who lacks means to meet his basic economic needs should be able to get money, promptly and equitably, through the public assistance program.

c. The amount of financial aid should be sufficient to maintain a living standard compatible with decency and health.

d. Public assistance should be administered with the same full respect for personal rights and responsibilities of needy individuals and families which society accords other members of the community.

e. Public assistance should be administered so as to assist individuals and families to regain the ability to meet their own basic needs. When this is not possible, each person and family should be assisted to function to maximum capacity.[75]

For the first time in the history of public welfare in this country, the rights of the client were specifically detailed. These included the right to:

a. apply for assistance;
b. adequate standards of relief;
c. appeal and a fair hearing;
d. confidentiality;
e. money payments;
f. equitable treatment; and

g. self-determination in relation both to receiving financial assistance and to using casework services.[76]

The impact of this legislation extended beyond the public assistance agency. The recognition of the legal right of the public welfare client who is on the bottom of the ladder, so to speak, appeared to extend to all clients in all types of agency settings. As this decade drew to a close, client self-determination in public welfare appeared close to becoming a reality. Clients were proposed for service on agency boards or advisory committees, bringing their own experiences and expertise to the problems and shortcomings of agency practices. Some clients had the opportunity to share in policy making and program development.[77]

ENDNOTES FOR CHAPTER 5

1   William H. Whyte, *The Organization Man*, (New York: Simon & Schuster, 1956).
2   *Brown v. Board of Education of Topeka*, 347 U.S. 483, 494 (1954).
3   The NASW was formed by the merger of the American Association of Social Workers, the American Association of Medical Social Workers, the National Association of School Social Workers, the American Association of Psychiatric Social Workers, the American Association of Group Workers, the Association for the Study of Community Organization, and the Social Work Research Group.
4   Ernest V. Hollis and Alice L. Taylor, *Social Work Education in the United States* (New York: Columbia University Press, 1951).
5   Werner W. Boehm, *Objectives of the Social Work Curriculum of the Future* (New York: Council on Social Work Education, 1959), p. 21.
6   Alfred Kadushin, "The Knowledge Base of Social Work," *Issues in American Social Work*, ed. Alfred J. Kahn (New York: Columbia University Press, 1959), p. 54.
7   Benjamin E. Youngdahl, "What We Believe," *The Social Welfare Forum: 1952* (New York: Columbia University Press, 1952), p. 31.
8   Adopted by the Delegate Assembly of the National Association of Social Workers, October 13, 1960.
9   Donald S. Howard, "Civil Liberties and Social Work," *The Social Welfare Forum: 1953* (New York: Columbia University Press, 1953), p. 40.
10 Arlien Johnson, "Educating Professional Social Workers for Ethical Practice," *Social Service Review*, June 1955, p. 126.

116   CLIENT SELF-DETERMINATION

11   Nathan E. Cohen, "The Place of the Sectarian Agency in Service to Groups," *The Social Welfare Forum: 1951* (New York: Columbia University Press, 1951), p. 271.
12   Howard, "Civil Liberties," p. 40.
13   Muriel W. Pumphrey, *The Teaching of Values and Ethics in Social Work Education* (New York: Council on Social Work Education, 1959), pp. 43-44.
14   Adopted by the Delegate Assembly of the National Association of Social Workers, October 13, 1960.
15   Walter A. Friedlander, *Concepts and Methods of Social Work* (Englewood Cliffs, NJ: Prentice-Hall, 1958), pp. 2-3.
16   Among the articles were: Saul Bernstein, "Self-Determination: King or Citizen in the Realm of Values?," *Social Work*, January 1960; Benjamin A. Gjenvick, "The Worker's Position with Respect to Client Self-Determination and Christian Responsibility," *Casework Papers, 1959* (New York: Family Service Association of America, 1959); Felix P. Biestek, "The Principle of Client Self-determination," *Social Casework*, November 1951; Helen Harris Perlman, "The Caseworker's Use of Collateral Information," *Social Welfare Forum: 1951* (New York: Columbia University Press, 1951).

The books were: Anita J. Faatz, *The Nature of Choice in Casework* (Chapel Hill: University of North Carolina Press, 1953); Felix P. Biestek, *The Principle of Client Self-Determination in Social Casework* (Washington, D.C.: Catholic University of America Press, 1951).
17   Perlman, "Caseworker's Use of Collateral Information," pp. 194-95.
18   Swithun Bowers, "Social Work and Human Problems," *Social Casework*, May 1954, p. 189.
19   Felix P. Biestek, *The Casework Relationship* (Chicago: Loyola University Press, 1957), p. 103.
20   Henry S. Maas, "Social Casework," *Concepts and Methods of Social Work*, ed. Walter A. Friedlander (Englewood Cliffs, NJ: Prentice-Hall, 1958), pp. 86-87.
21   Friedlander, *Concepts and Methods*, p. 3; Herbert Bisno, *The Philosophy of Social Work* (Washington, D.C.: Public Affairs Press, 1952), p. 96; Gordon Hamilton, *Theory and Practice of Social Casework*, 2nd ed. (New York: Columbia University Press, 1951), p. 44.
22   Friedlander, *Concepts and Methods*, p. 3; Leonard Mayo, "Presidential Address," *Trends in Social Work*, ed. Frank J. Bruno, 2nd ed. (New York: Columbia University Press, 1957), p. 370; Arthur P. Miles, *American Social Work Theory* (New York: Harper and Brothers, 1954), p. 33.
23   Martha Branscombe, "Basic Policies and Principles of Public Child Care Service," *Social Welfare Forum: 1951* (New York: Columbia University Press, 1951), pp. 336-37.

24 Friedlander, *Concepts and Methods,* p. 3.

25 Biestek, "Client Self-Determination," p. 372.

26 Perlman, "Caseworker's Use of Collateral Information," p. 195.

27 Ibid.

28 Ibid.

29 Elliot Studt, "An Outline for Study of Social Authority Factors in Casework," *Social Casework,* June 1954, pp. 231-32; Samuel Mencher, "The Concept of Authority and Social Casework," *Casework Papers: 1960* (New York: Family Service Association of America, 1960), p. 126.

30 "Notes and Comments: Public Assistance—Straws in the Wind," *Social Service Review,* March 1956, p. 75.

31 Margaret Hickey, "Presidential Address," *Social Welfare Forum: 1957* (New York: Columbia University Press, 1957), p. 6.

32 Herman D. Stein and Richard A. Cloward, *Social Perspectives on Behavior* (Glencoe, IL: The Free Press, 1958); Grace Longwell Coyle, "The Bridge Between Social Work and the Social Sciences," *The Social Welfare Forum: 1958* (New York: Columbia University Press, 1958), pp. 216-38; Brook Chisholm "World Mental Health," *The Social Welfare Forum: 1960* (New York: Columbia University Press, 1960), pp. 42-53; David Landy, "Problems of the Person Seeking Help in Our Culture," *The Social Welfare Forum: 1960* (New York: Columbia University Press, 1960), pp. 127-45; Florence R. Kluckholm,"Dominant and Variant Cultural Value Orientations," *The Social Welfare Forum: 1951* (New York: Columbia University Press, 1951), pp. 97-113; Paul Barrabee, "How Cultural Factors Affect Family Life," *The Social Welfare Forum: 1954* (New York: Columbia University Press, 1954), pp. 17-30; Irving Weisman and Jacob Chwast, "Control and Values in Social Work Treatment," *Social Casework,* November 1970, pp. 451-56.

33 Barrabee, "Cultural Factors," p. 17.

34 Weisman and Chwast, "Control and Values," p. 455.

35 Isabel Stamm, "Ego Psychology," *Issues in American Social Work,* ed. Alfred Kahn (New York: Columbia University Press, 1959), p. 80 ff.

36 Vera S. Margolis, "Ego Centered Treatment of the Adolescent Girl," *Casework Papers, 1956* (New York: Family Service Association in America, 1956), pp. 100, 106.

37 Charlotte S. Henry, "Initiating Service with the Non-Voluntary Client," *Casework Papers, 1958* (New York: Family Service Association of America, 1958), pp. 144-146; Hanna Grunwald, "Group Counseling with the Multi-problem Family," *The Use of Group Techniques in the Family Agency* (New York: Family Service Association of America, 1959), p. 33.

38 Leon Eisenberg, "The Family in the Mid-Twentieth Century," *The Social Welfare Forum: 1960* (New York: Columbia University Press, 1960), p. 105.

39 Kermit Wiltse, "The 'Hopeless' Family," *The Social Welfare Forum: 1958* (New York: Columbia University Press, 1958), p. 137.

40 Alfred Kadushin, "Opposition to Referral for Psychiatric Treatment," *Social Work*, April 1957, p. 79.

41 Walter Hass, "Reaching Out—A Dynamic Concept in Casework," *Social Work*, July 1959, p. 44.

42 Ibid., p. 43.

43 Helen Harris Perlman, "Social Casework: The Problem Solving Approach," *Encyclopedia of Social Work*, 16th ed. (New York: National Association of Social Workers, 1971), p. 1207.

44 Ibid., p. 1209.

45 Ibid., p. 1207.

46 Helen Harris Perlman, "The Client's Treatability," *Social Work*, October 1956, p. 33.

47 Irving Kaufman, "Understanding the Dynamics of Parents with Character Disorders," *Casework Papers, 1960* (New York: Family Service Association of America, 1960), p. 10.

48 Robert K. Taylor, "Identification and Ego-Directive Casework," *Social Work*, January 1960, p. 45.

49 Ibid.

50 Gladys E. Townsend, "Short-term Casework with Clients Under Stress," *Social Casework*, November, 1953, p. 395.

51 "Definition of the Function of the Group Worker," American Association of Group Workers, 1948.

52 Raymond Fisher, "Social Group Work in Group Service Agencies," *Social Work with Groups, 1959* (New York: National Association of Social Workers, 1959), p. 21.

53 American Association of Group Workers, cited in Nathan E. Cohen, "Implications of the Present Scene for Social Group Work Practice," *The Social Welfare Forum: 1955* (New York: Columbia University Press, 1955), p. 57.

54 Gisela Knopka, "The Generic and the Specific in Group Work Practice in the Psychiatric Setting," *Social Work*, January 1956, p. 77.

55 Gertrude Wilson and Gladys Ryland, "Social Classes: Implications for Social Group Work," *The Social Welfare Forum: 1954* (New York: Columbia University Press, 1954), p. 171.

56 Nathan E. Cohen, "Reversing the Process of Social Disorganization," *Issues in American Social Work*, ed. by A. Kahn (New York: Columbia University Press, 1959), p. 139.

57 Campbell G. Murphy, "Community Organization for Social Welfare," *The Social Work Year Book, 1957* (New York: National Association of Social Workers, 1957), p. 179.

58 Charles E. Hendry, "Community Organization Teamwork in Rural

Communities," *The Social Welfare Forum: 1953* (New York: Columbia University Press, 1953), p. 271.

59 Cohen, "Reversing the Process," pp. 139-40.

60 Chauncey A. Alexander and Charles McCann, "The Concept of Representativeness in Community Organization," *Social Work,* January 1956, p. 48.

61 Mildred C. Barry, "Current Concepts in Community Organization," *Group Work and Community Organization, 1956* (New York: Columbia University Press, 1956), p. 11.

62 Alexander and McCann, "Concept of Representatives," p. 48.

63 Violet M. Seider, "What is Community Organization Practice in Social Work?," *The Social Welfare Forum: 1956* (New York: Columbia University Press, 1956), p. 172.

64 Leonard W. Mayo, "Community Planning for Health and Welfare," *The Social Welfare Forum: 1952* (New York: Columbia University Press, 1952), p. 231.

65 Anne Goodman, "Medical Social Work with the Aged in a Public Insitution," *Social Casework,* November 1955, p. 418.

66 Erving Goffman, *Asylums* (Garden City, NY: Anchor Books, 1961).

67 Ken Kesey, *One Flew Over the Cuckoo's Nest* (New York: Viking Press, 1962).

68 Hortense S. Cochrane, "Discussion of Casework Service Today in Institutions for Delinquents," *Selected Papers in Social Casework: 1951* (Raleigh, NC: Health Publications Institute, Inc., 1951), p. 114.

69 William G. Nagel, "Custody and Treatment-Twin Aims of the Prison Social Worker," *Casework Papers, 1957* (New York: Family Service Association of America, 1957), p. 91 ff.

70 Norman V. Lourie, "The Children's Institution: One Step in Casework Treatment," *The Social Welfare Forum: 1954* (New York: Columbia University Press, 1954), p. 145.

71 Elliot Studt, "Learning Casework in a Juvenile Probation Setting," *Social Casework,* October 1951, p. 345.

72 Herman Piven and Donnell M. Pappenfort, "Strain Between Administration and Worker: A View From the Field of Corrections," *Social Work,* October 1960, p. 40.

73 Mary B. Colvert, "Current Emphases in Casework in Public Agencies in Rural Areas," *Selected Papers in Social Casework: 1951* (Raleigh, NC: Health Publications Institute, Inc., 1951), pp. 56-57.

74 Crystal M. Potter, "Constructive Aspects of Public Assistance for Children," *Selected Papers in Social Casework: 1951* (Raleigh, NC: Health Publications Institute, Inc., 1951), p. 65.

75 Joint statement by the Bureau of Public Assistance and the American Public Welfare Association prepared for the Council on Social Work

Education, January 1958.

76 Eunice Minton, "Services for Children in Public Assistance," *Casework Papers, 1957* (New York: Family Service Association of America, 1957), p. 74; Eunice Minton, "Effect of Setting on Casework Practice in Public Assistance," *Social Casework*, February 1956, p. 65; Robert H. MacRae, "Prerequisite for Strong Family Life," *The Social Welfare Forum: 1958* (New York.: Columbia University Press, 1958), p. 117.

77 Frances Levinson Bateman, "How do Professional Workers Become Professional?," *Casework Papers: 1956* (New York: Family Service Association of America, 1956), p. 36.

_____ Widespread turbulence in the decade
_____ Theory _____Values and
self-determination _____Practice _____
_____ Civil rights struggle _____ Right
to public assistance _____Right to
dissent _____Behavioral modification

CHAPTER 6

1960—1969   PART I

IT WAS a time of intense feelings, protest, violence, and re-
definition of values.

This was a decade of three presidents, John F. Kennedy
(1961-1963), Lyndon B. Johnson (1963-1969), and Richard M.
Nixon (1969-1974). It saw the United States enter the longest
period of sustained economic growth in modern history. It was
the decade in which one president laid the foundation for the
"War on Poverty," the second tried to implement it, and the
third apparently set about to dismantle it.

The Kennedy years were identified by sharp contrasts, both
on the foreign and domestic scenes. They were years of anxiety
as Americans heard about the Cold War, the Berlin Crisis, the
Bay of Pigs Invasion and felt ever so close to the brink of war as
television unfolded the drama of the Cuban Missile Crisis—the

confrontation of two world powers, the Soviet Union and the United States.

During Kennedy's administration, through the medium of television, the nation experienced the thrill of Commander Alan B. Shephard's suborbital flight in space, the suspense and fear of the civil rights marches, and the intense grief at the assassination of the President.

It was into President Johnson's hands that "the torch was passed" on that fateful day in Dallas. Johnson was a strong personality who provided confidence and assurance at a time when the country needed both. He set into motion the necessary legislation for establishing the "Great Society," with its liberal welfare programs. These years brought increased domestic attention to the social ills of the American people. Despite new benefits, the establishment of medicare, and landmark civil rights legislation, matters grew worse. Riots occurred in the cities of Newark, Los Angeles, Chicago, and Detroit. The Reverend Martin Luther King, Jr., civil rights leader and advocate of nonviolent strategies, was murdered in Memphis, Tennessee. Two months later Robert Kennedy was assassinated while engaged in his presidential campaign.

During this decade the war in Viet Nam intensified. Increased United States involvement brought severe criticism of President Johnson and his foreign policies. The protest so intensified that he chose not to run for reelection.

Johnson's successor was Richard Nixon. Nixon was elected on the platform that he would restore "law and order." During the early years of his administration, the government appeared to undergo rapid change. Many of the domestic programs of the prior administration were dismantled or delayed.

In the latter part of this decade, the profession of social work functioned within an atmosphere of discontent, disappointment, and suspicion. Optimism and hope changed into despair. The federal administration, critical of social workers, chastised them by urging that they go and seek "honest" work.[1]

Also in these years, there were calls for the profession to be relevant to the needs of the people, to consider accountability as a criterion of evaluation, and to revitalize social action as an effective and appropriate social work technique. Increased awareness of the need for professional research and serious evaluation of treatment models and techniques were also a part of this decade.

During the sixties the casework frame of reference expanded so that it now included the functional model, the problem-solving model, the psycho-social model, and the behavioral modification model. Increased attention was given to the use of group work, and intervention at the societal level once again became a significant concern of social work.

Within the profession the focus appeared to change from one primarily centered upon the individual to one concerned with broader social realities. This shift required the profession to reconsider its philosophical beliefs, and though client self-determination continued to be recognized and respected, it did not remain unchallenged.

THEORY

The social work profession, concerned with social injustice and civil rights, scrutinized the democratic philosophy of both the country and the profession. There was increased sensitivity to the rights and responsibilities of the citizen-client. Criticism was raised regarding those practices and procedures which humiliated, stigmatized, demoralized, and punished the people called clients. As the profession reassessed civil liberties and clients' rights in the day to day practice of social work, a new sense of direction and commitment emerged.

> I invite you to listen to the changing vocabulary of social work. The thrust is from passive to active voice, from past imperfect to present imperative tense, from ideas of adjustment to those of coping, from social workers as enablers to social workers as change agents, from client as having self-determination to client as change target, from compromise to manipulation of power, from coordination to innovation. I do not mean that all these are antithetical ideas or that in other guises they have not figured in

social work considerations before. But the words have consequences and the emphasis on the aggressive, innovative, intrusive
mode is strong among us now; it reveals our press and
inclination.[2]

1. *Value Issues*. The value issues inherent in social work, such
as the nature of man, human motivation, freedom, rights and
responsibilities, became deep concerns. How could social work
preserve the democratic heritage in a society beset by social
problems of potentially disastrous proportions? The task was
not an easy one.

> What we struggle for today is the preservation of the conscious
> awareness that each individual human being is precious, with
> inviolable rights, and measures which will support and increase
> man's freedom and well-being under changing social conditions
> and national and world-wide dangers.[3]

> It is one thing to believe in wide democratic participation as a
> value or philosophy. It is quite another to have a coherent set of
> theories about what constitutes participation in diverse condi-
> tions, how it affects the goal we set for ourselves, how varying but
> typical real life situations affect participation.[4]

The extensiveness of this dilemma can be seen in the many
articles on this issue which appeared during the decade. For
example, while a number of major social work textbooks
expressed no problems about the principle of client self-
determination,[5] a few writers saw the need to clarify the relationship of client self-determination to other social values.[6]
Speaking to this point, Gyarfas referred to a qualified self-determination, limited in degree by two factors—"the worker's
diagnosis" and "the varying rights and responsibilities" of the
client.[7]

The worker was described as being "the final arbiter" in
determining what would be in the best interests of the client, for
as Greenwood observed:

> In a professional relationship, however, the professional dictates
> what is good and evil for the client, who has no choice but to

accept the "professional judgment." Obviously, this is a different view of professional attitude.[8]

On the surface, this position appears to be opposed to the principle of client self-determination. But if one recalls the discussion of authority of the preceding decades, the worker's authority was considered to be derived from his professional knowledge and skills. The worker was cautioned to use this authority carefully, wisely, always mindful of the needs, goals, and rights of the client. If the relationship between client and worker is a true partnership, with client and worker being coequals, the point of the worker "dictating" and of the client having "no choice" becomes invalid.

2. *Inherent Problems.* Other problems also appeared as the principle of client self-determination was further refined during this decade. They included problems which

- pertained to making choices between alternative values;
- related to the concept of self-determination;[9]
- were associated with inequities in the availability of alternatives;
- pertained to the capacities—emotional, social and physical—of the individual necessary for making a decision;
- were associated with the contrast between self-determination as a principle and as a therapeutic technique;
- involved agency purpose, structure and function; and
- were associated with the client-worker relationship and the knowledge and skill of the social worker.[10]

Inherent in some of these problem areas were matters of the relative weight of certain value choices. In helping the client to see the possible alternatives, the identification of choices as good, better, or best implies certain value weights. These, however, can only be measured from the client's situation and circumstances. Yet assessment, risk-taking, and the evaluation of consequences of certain decisions require the active participation of the social worker as the helping agent.

To some, this activity of the worker seemed to be a disguised euphemism for worker control. The worker was expected to maintain a sense of balance between a laissez-faire, nondirective attitude on the one hand and a highly authoritarian controlling attitude on the other.

3. *Reevaluation of Self-Determination.* Faced with these problems, the profession began to wonder if it had a principle called client self-determination. Alan Keith-Lucas identified several components of the principle itself. He observed that there was an element which he labeled "the principle of noninterference except in essentials." This accepted the premise of the client having the right to make his own decisions until he demonstrated that continuance of this right would be detrimental to himself and others. The worker's responsibility then would be to intervene on the client's behalf. This was not in violation of the client's rights, but rather represented professionally responsible behavior.[11]

Another component associated with the principle was that of "contractual limitation." The social work relationship was considered a contract between the client and the worker, wherein the client retained the final decision-making power unless his rights had been suspended by law. However, even in this instance, the role of the social worker was to protect the rights of the client under provision of "due process." The caution suggested by Keith-Lucas was that while the client has a right and a need to make his choices, and ought to do so, there was no firm assurance that he would necessarily do so.[12]

A new dimension seemed to be added to the principle of client self-determination at this juncture. Soyer proposed that within self-determination the client had a corresponding right to make bad choices, that is, the right to fail. The experience of failing need not be viewed as being detrimental to the client but rather, in and of itself, could have positive potentials for the client.

> This is how all people grow, how they gain a more mature view of themselves and the world. They succeed and fail and through success and failure they learn[13]

It is the life experience itself with its success, failure, and in between that is what really enables the client to evaluate himself, and in the end, to set his goals realistically.[14]

4. *Existential Philosophy* With the introduction of existential philosophy to the profession, other facets of self-determination were highlighted. In the latter half of the sixties articles appeared which suggested that social work, with its historical championing of the right of each individual to "choose his own destiny and to assume responsibility for his choice," was, in effect, implementing the fundamental tenets of existentialism.[15]

In this unpredictable world in which nothing is preordained, man is faced with the necessity for constant decision-making. This fundamental characteristic may be grasped in Kierkegaard's philosophical commitment to freedom and value as inherent in individual man. "Each individual is confronted with ethical choices which he alone can make and for which he assumes full responsibility." The set of choices does not terminate in that choice since "every decision an individual makes is irrevocable and presents him with the necessity for subsequent decisions." Man alone realizes this intrinsic attribute of choice. He alone achieves freedom. He alone is faced fully with the consequences of freedom . . . . Man is not only ultimately but totally responsible for the world.[16]

This discussion caused social work to refine its understanding of the nature of the self and its capacity for freedom. Krill, in speaking of the nature of the self, observed that the self is "never a fixed, closed, totally predetermined form," rather it is a constant process of growth and change. So persons too are in that state of "becoming" as they draw upon their past knowledge and experiences and direct their future guided by their goals, providing their "own unique assessment of the duties, responsibilities, and inner prompting . . . ."[17]

Within the existential context, freedom is defined as the ability of the individual to rise above the "powerful negative driving forces" in his daily living. Through the social work relationship, the client is able to identify "actual, reality-based choices" and in turn to discover satisfaction through asserting himself as a free being.[18]

But in considering the existential position, a caution appeared necessary. Does it exaggerate the individual's right to freedom? Does it mean total freedom without concern for the rights of others, without regard for social responsibility? Fully developed, the existential point of view, according to some of its critics, could be understood to sanction complete absolution of the individual from social responsibilities and to advocate an aggressive "survival of the fittest" approach to life.

5. *The Three Conferences.* The inquiry into the philosophical basis of social work was quite extensive as evidenced by the three major conferences in this period dealing with social work values. In 1965 the National Association of Social Workers sponsored a Regional Institute on the theme "Values in Social Work: A Re-Examination." The following year, the Council on Social Work Education cosponsored a conference, "An Intercultural Exploration: Universals and Differences in Social Work Values, Functions, and Practice." The third conference held in 1968 under the leadership of the International Conference on Social Welfare, commemorated the twentieth anniversary of the United Nations *Universal Declaration of Human Rights,* and focused on "Social Welfare and Human Rights."

In these three conferences, the innate dignity and worth of the individual and his right to be self-determining were consistently reaffirmed. The individual and society were viewed as interrelated and interdependent. Events which positively or negatively affected one, led to change on the other. For example, if an individual was denied his right to self-determination, not only did he suffer but so did society. In these conferences social responsibility was seen as a corollary of social rights, and social welfare the antecedent of social justice. Social justice supported the claim of one's civil rights.

At the NASW conference, a number of social work theorists discussed the value issues in general and client self-determination in particular.

The keynote speaker dealt with the basic value assumptions of self-determination, the interrelatedness of the individual and society, the mutuality of needs, obligations, and responsibilities between the individual and his society. The individual's claim to his freedom of choice is founded upon his legitimate right as a citizen, upon his basic human needs, and upon his natural thrust for need satisfaction. This is basic to social functioning. Society is obligated to promote the well-being of the individual, and to facilitate his self-fulfillment. In return, society can anticipate that it will be enriched by the many, varied contributions of its people "in proportion to their abilities and resources. Man and society are interdependent partners together in this effort; both have duties and responsibilities to perform."[19]

It is in this conference that one finds legitimate rights extended beyond the confines of civil law, a theme to be more fully developed in the subsequent conferences.

Any discussion of value implementation needs to be prefaced by a consideration of four major problems: determination of value priorities, the need to clarify the confusion between the concepts "preferable and preferred," the controversy over the existence of absolute values, and the value conflicts associated with diverse philosophies of life.[20]

Addressing himself to the problem of identifying values, Chakerian cautioned that the concept of value "remains, at best, somewhat vague." What is a common concern, however, are the "purposes, goals, and criteria inherent in judgment and behavior."[21] Differences of values among people ought to be anticipated and accepted as such, despite the fact that such variation leads to a complex, often confusing, state of affairs. Chakerian particularly emphasized that

- values are expressions of selfhood which are constitutionally and culturally derived;
- values, although they may be varied and lack uniformity, are interrelated;
- no facet of human behavior is free from value judgments; and

- values are part of life situations and involve emotional commitment.[22]

Helen Harris Perlman associated the dilemma of values with two critical problems in today's American society; the problem of "other-directedness" (that is, man being responsive to external cues and signals from other than his own counsel), and the problem of "identity-confusion" (the individual assessing his identity through the mirror offered by the reaction of others).[23]

In a person's search for identity, Perlman's position parallels the existentialists' concept of self: "I *am* because I *will*." This is the essence of self-determination: "I am because I will to choose, to decide, to be responsible for, a cause of, the consequences that follow on my actions."[24] As every individual is seen to be a part of many groups, each in turn serves to mold and shape him. Nevertheless he remains a unique being, a person of dignity and worth.

Social work, then, it seemed to her, had two alternatives regarding the principle of client self-determination: either to reject self-determination because it is not viable, or to accept self-determination and live within the reality of its limitations. She preferred reality.

> If we reject self-determination as a viable means and end, if we deny its inherence in everyday transaction between ourselves and those we profess to help, then what do we choose as a workable psychology and philosophy in its place? What alternatives are there? These, in brief: a dehumanized view of man and animal or machine; a view of choice and responsibility as the right of some governing few—the Fascist concept, or, at its opposite pole, a state of anarchy; a view of robots manipulating other robots to the predetermined whims or plans of powerholders; a view, in short, that is intolerable to entertain....

> Self-determination, then, is the expression of our innate drive to experience the self as cause, as master of oneself. Its practical everyday exercise builds into man's maturational process because it requires the recognition of the actual, the consideration of the possible, and in the light of these . . . the adaptation involved in decision and choice. Self-determination is based on a realistic

view of freedom. Freedom, in essence, is the inner capacity and outer opportunity to make reasoned choices among possible, socially acceptable alternatives. True, each man's exercise of self-determination is predetermined and limited by his nature and nurture, by past and present people and circumstances, and by his society's prevailing commitments to humanistic ideals. Yet, within all these uniquely individual boundaries and within a larger society much as ours, which forges chains even as it speaks for liberty, within these paradoxes, we must help man to find in himself some wish and power to be captain of his soul and master of his fate . . . . As we do this we build into each man a sense of himself as a person and affirm his worth as a human being. This one part reality in the stubborn human illusion about self-determination is palpable and vital, ready for its potentials to be plumbed and realized.[25]

Saul Bernstein attempted to clarify three distinct aspects of self-determination:

- as a need or drive of people in our society;
- as a methodological concept or process by which the individual is free to make intelligent decisions; and
- as a value, a goal, an end to be desired.[26]

Although these appear to be distinctive, they are interrelated and overlap and create conflict over priorities, goals, and methods. Social workers should not avoid this kind of conflict because out of it might come a productive opportunity for change, implied Bernstein.

Keith-Lucas examined the change in the principle of self-determination itself. He insisted that the principle be viewed as a dynamic concept, responsive to many change situations including change which occurs within the society and that which is brought about by conflict and confrontation. Change might also be associated with new knowledge which broadens the theory and method base of social work. Change became visible as the client was viewed as the initiator of service, rather than the one who was acted upon by the professional or who was affected by things beyond his control. Finally, change can be a consequence of the varying conceptions of the role of the worker.

The source of these changes is found in increased understanding of human needs, in the basic belief that social workers know much more about people, their behavior, and their social relationships than before, and in the fact that as a profession social work is also changing. Keith-Lucas cautioned against the danger of the social worker himself becoming more conservative, tradition-bound, and less a dynamic force for change.[27]

An underlying theme that emerged from this conference was the issue of individual freedom versus social responsibility. A hope was expressed that at least as an initial step, the issue be redefined to read:

> This measuring of the individual must be tied indissolubly with a belief in social responsibility, with the conviction that self-determination and self-fulfillment can only be achieved in the kind of social order that demands social obligation, and social responsibility as the essential climate for each individual to realize himself. There can be no self-determination without concern for the common good . . . . The task of mediating, conciliating, integrating, arbitrating between the self and society is the creative opportunity of social work. What task could be more exciting, more rewarding, more self-fulfilling? It is the task of building a free society and freeing man to live within it.[28]

The second of the three conferences, the one sponsored by the Council on Social Work Education, focused on the problem of universals and differences in social work values, functions, and practice. Several observations were made regarding the problems of values in social work. For example, the conference attempted to distinguish between normative values and instrumental values. Normative values are defined as goals or ends. Instrumental values were the means of actions necessary to attain those goals. Instrumental values may be transitional, reflecting the quality of change, while normative values connote "strong belief and a quality of absoluteness."[29]

This conference identified some problems related to the concepts of universal values, value conflict, and value violation.

Universal values needed to be classified and their distinctiveness highlighted. To do so, these guidelines were developed:

a. A value remains a value even when it is violated.
b. Absolute *consistency* and the lack of conflict are not the criteria of values.
c. One should look for *ideational influences* which predispose individuals towards certain types of action and look for purity or totality.
d. Dominance of a value and universality are not the same.[30]
e. Social work involves dealing with a multiplexity of value mixtures. How these are refined is demonstrated in the principle of individualization.[31]

While this conference did not go beyond the raising of questions, a hope was expressed that the exploration of the depth and the ramifications of the value dimension in social work practice would be a continuing process.

Some critical questions regarding self-determination were raised for future consideration:

• What political, educational, and other values are involved in what might be called the dilemma of self-determination?
• Should self-determination be thought of, not as a value, but rather as a descriptive term, one that may describe states of mind that are really quite different?
• Do the concepts "self-help," "self-determination," and "self-direction" have the same meaning?
• Does the manner of applying self-determination create a particular approach to practice?
• Do social workers apply the principle because they have to or because people will not let them do anything else?
• Are methodological and value components inextricably mixed in the method of self-determination?[32]

This conference ended on the note that values are "tricky things"—tricky in that all social behavior is related to values. They serve as guiding forces, not visible, but like gravity or centrifugal force, they are believed to exist "because without assuming it, we cannot account for the data." Values provide order and direction; they assist in making "understandable," "coherent," and "sometimes predictable" what otherwise would appear to be "chaotic" and "uncomprehensive." Yet they remain elusive, as underlying standards of judgment, and are difficult to "capture within a concept."[33]

The third conference on values developed the theme: "Social Welfare and Human Rights." The main purpose of the conference was to evaluate the progress which had been made in the international community since the *Declaration of Human Rights* had been set forth by the United Nations in 1948. It also attempted to redefine human rights in the "light of changing political and economic conditions."[34]

The conference recognized that in any nation, human rights are governed by three factors: (1) "The national goals, aims, and values; (2) the institutional and political framework of the government; and (3) the stage of the country's economic development." It noted that any change which attempted to "improve, advance, and protect" human rights was bound to create stress and a state of tension, especially as one attempted to relate human needs to governmental priorities, resources, and programs. Government and citizens together have mutual concerns involving them in a symbiotic relationship, a state of mutual dependency. Beneficial change with regard to citizens' rights and well-being is also a benefit to the nation. Conversely, change which is detrimental or harmful to the citizen is equally disadvantageous to the well-being of the nation.[35]

The conference sought to relate the relationship of the rights of the individual expressed in the *Universal Declaration of Human Rights* to the rights of society and the nation. To this end, social welfare was viewed as a basic means in securing the rights of both the individual and society. Concomitant with the recognition of rights was the acceptance of obligations inherent in them. Rights and duties were inseparable and social welfare was "a basic tool" in securing these human rights.

Advocacy of rights without advocacy of duties is nonproductive. A mature understanding of the interdependency of rights and duties, and of the individual and society, is an important requisite for bringing into realization the goals of freedom, justice, equality, and well-being.[36]

Someone observed that rights are seldom freely given to an individual; rather they must be wrestled from counter-value forces. It was recognized in this conference that a combination of factors could interfere with, or prevent the securing of these basic rights.

    a. Some might be complex factors, rooted in tradition, culture, or history.

    b. Some are factors steeped in fear and prejudice.

    c. Some could be the result of exploitation and the workshop of power and property.

    d. Some appear to be illogical and related to bureaucratic obstacles.

    e. Some center on political guile and economic self-interest, rather than on human concern.

    f. Some can be the consequences of uneven national development.[37]

Social justice and social welfare were viewed as essential, interrelated parts of a nation's social and economic development. Social welfare involves many activities and functions directed towards the promotion of social well-being. It increases the choices which an individual can make to realize his human rights.[38] The provisions for the social well-being of the citizenry was only a part of government's role in social welfare. Additionally, it ought to provide opportunities for the exercise of self-determination, as a necessary component of social welfare policies and practices in any country. By assuming the right of the citizen to be self-determining, the concept of social justice would, to that extent, be promoted.

The conference sought to clarify the intent of the *Universal Declaration* by identifying the pertinent rights. These were seen to include the right to social security, to relief payments, to services, and to participate in decisions. Subsequently, these rights were expanded to include the right to life, to justice, to housing, to *habeas corpus*, to work, to equal pay, and to education. These resulted from two "new" rights: social rights to development and the right to participate actively in the process of development. The right to participate was an important right, based upon one's right "to be considered a person, conscientious and responsible, able to function as a human being and as an agent" in the change process. The right of participation was characterized as "a natural and responsible claim made by human beings."[39]

This right of participation was important for several reasons:

a. The decisions and the programs are enriched when more people know about them and when more people can share their experience.

b. There is a greater chance of meeting real needs, of being more efficient.

c. The person who is involved in the decisions becomes more interested and related to their implementation. (He does not have to be convinced.)

d. When passivity is replaced by participation, the interested persons are given the opportunity to increase their knowledge and to improve their competence.

e. Participation is an important tool in fighting conformity, passivism, the spirit of dependency, and stagnation.[40]

From this vantage point, social rights and civil rights were viewed as connected, both essential to the individual's right to dignity. Self-respect, the respect for others, equality, and self-determination were woven together as the "essence of human dignity." Civil rights which are in harmony with social rights create a state of social justice; this in turn is an "expression of human brotherhood." Unfortunately, as Hanart concluded, "To set up human rights is one thing, to make them effective (is) quite another."[41]

PRACTICE

1. *Client Self-Determination as a Political Consideration.* As social work struggled with the philosophical and theoretical discussions of the principle of client self-determination, it also faced the problems of securing and augmenting this principle in the form of civil and social rights. This political dimension was necessary for the establishment and maintenance of social justice. If an individual is to develop his potentialities to their fullest capacity, this must occur within a society where social rights are recognized and social justice is a reality.

In terms of civil rights, the decade of the sixties was characterized by turbulence and strife. "Picketing, marches, boycotts, religious assemblies, freedom rides and sit-ins" were as much a part of the reality of this decade as were bombings, beatings, bloodshed, and bullets.[42] Black and white, rich and poor, young and old together joined hands to wage war against the forces of inequality, prejudice, discrimination, and injustice. These forces attempted to actualize the promise of democracy for all people, not for just the privileged few.

Out of this activity, social justice emerged as an essential prerequisite for the exercise of freedom of choice. Freedom to choose what? Many times the answer to this question was sought on the streets and in the courts. In attempting to identify this *what*, it was discovered that many rights were abused, neglected, or violated. Each violation subtracted from the freedom of everyone. The endangered rights were: the right to financial assistance; to equality of opportunity in education, housing, and employment; to freedom of movement; to choice in family planning; to access to legal rights of due process, including fair and equitable treatment; to counsel, to a hearing, and to appeal; to health and freedom from hunger; to privacy and to confidentiality; and the right to life itself.

As these rights were identified, the line of distinction between civil and social rights became blurred. Common threads were contained in these rights and were found in the dignity and worth of the individual and his exercise of the right to freedom of choice.

In the social work literature of this decade the issue of rights often surfaced as a consequence of gross abuse and violations, which then served as a catalyst for demands of reform. Through this discussion of the rights of the client, especially of the public welfare client, various assumed rights eventually became legal, civil rights via court decisions.

2. *Self-Determination and the Right of Assistance.* The authors of the 1935 Social Security Act established a principle which was new for this country—that of legally enforceable entitlement to social security and public assistance. This established the legal precedent for the public welfare client to claim his right to public funds, to equality of treatment, and to appeal if discriminated against.

Change comes about very often in response to crisis situations. During this decade there were several crises in social work which attracted national attention. Through the broad discussion of the issues came subsequent legislative modifications. Each change was the product of someone's personal hardship. Each legislative victory was built upon human suffering.

The first crisis situation with which we are concerned occurred in Newburgh, New York. In 1961 the City Council, as administrator of public assistance, instituted a program to tighten the eligibility requirements for public assistance. This program was criticized as being punitive to the client and a violation of his civil rights, especially the right to due process. The Council's position was that this program was necessary because of the rising costs of maintaining Newburgh's public assistance program. Newburgh had experienced an increase in the nonwhite population, due largely to migration from the South. The nonwhite population had almost tripled in the ten years, 1950-1960. The official stance was that although Newburgh had only five percent of its population on public assistance, it was spending one-sixth of its budget for its welfare program.[43] Thus the stage was set for a major confrontation in public welfare. "On May 1, the city manager of Newburgh ordered assistance recipients to appear before the police for questioning or lose their grants."[44]

As a consequence of this order, the State Welfare Department notified Newburgh that it faced the loss of both state and federal funds and that its order was illegal.[45]

The City Council responded by supporting the city manager, and accused the state of interference in local matters. They then issued a program of restrictive rules. These rules sought to deny funds to "unfit" mothers, to reduce the amount of assistance grants, to severely limit grants to newcomers, and to establish a suitable residency requirement. The thirteen rules were:

1. All cash payment which can be converted to food, clothing, and rent vouchers and the like without basic harm to the intent of the aid shall be issued in voucher form henceforth.

2. All able-bodied adult males on relief of any kind who are capable of working are to be assigned to the chief of building maintenance for work assignment on a forty-hour week.

3. All recipients physically capable of and available for private employment who are offered a job but refuse it, regardless of the type of employment involved, are to be denied relief.

4. All mothers of illegitimate children are to be advised that should they have any more children out of wedlock, they shall be denied relief.

5. All applicants for relief who have left a job voluntarily, that is, who have not been fired or laid off, shall be denied relief.

6. The allotment for any one family unit shall not exceed the take-home pay of the lowest city employee with a family of a comparable size. Also, no relief shall be granted to any family whose income is in excess of the latter figure.

7. All files of all Aid to Dependent Children cases are to be brought to the office of the corporation counsel for review monthly. All new cases of any kind will be referred to the corporation counsel prior to certification of payment.

8. All applicants for relief who are new to the city must show evidence that their plans in coming to the city involved a concrete offer of employment, similar to that required of foreign immigrants. All such persons shall be limited to two weeks of relief. Those who cannot show evidence shall be limited to one week of relief.

9. Aid to persons except the aged, blind, and disabled shall be limited to three months in any one year.

10. All recipients, except those who are disabled, blind, non-ambulatory, or otherwise incapacitated, shall report to the Department of Public Welfare monthly for a conference regarding the status of their case.

11. Once the budget for the fiscal year is approved by the Council, it shall not be exceeded by the Welfare Department unless approved by Council for supplemental appropriation.

12. There shall be a monthly expenditure limit on all categories of welfare aid. This monthly expenditure limit shall be established by the Department of Public Welfare at the time of presenting the budget, and shall take into account seasonal variations.

13. Prior to certifying or continuing any more aid to dependent cases, a determination shall be made as to the home environment. If the home environment is not satisfactory, the children in that home shall be placed in foster care in lieu of welfare aid to the family adults.[46]

Of the thirteen regulations, eleven were ultimately declared illegal. The battle drew national attention as reflected in a *New York Times* editorial:

Cruelty anywhere is the concern of mankind everywhere. The city of Newburgh, New York, should not be surprised at finding itself famous overnight for writing its own rules for dispensation of welfare grants to the needy.

The State and federal governments, supplying a considerable percentage of the money, have a legal as well as moral interest in standards. Albany has always been timid in asserting its disciplinary power to correct local deficiencies, but the State Board of Social Welfare will hold a public hearing July 7 to investigate the Newburgh situation.

The state has a duty to help in Newburgh as well as forbid cruel and unusual punishments for the crime of being poor. Newburgh, enjoying know-nothing applause from near and far for "getting tough" on the needy must be made by the State to realize that it is not a law unto itself. We suppose a good many cities would like to order their masses of poor out of town by sundown, or week's end. But what if everybody did that?[47]

The crisis continued through the summer and Newburgh's City Council was finally forced to modify its program. The significance of the Newburgh Crisis was the congressional attention it aroused. This resulted in the *1962 Public Welfare Amendments* which established new welfare guidelines, making it mandatory for states as recipients of federal funds to adopt the following policies.

1. Prohibit practices that violate the individual's privacy or personal dignity, or harass him, or violate his constitutional rights.

2. Require that assistance be given promptly and continued regularly until the individual is found to be ineligible.

3. Prohibit the practice of assuming that a recipient of public assistance receives some regular income from relatives or other sources and subtracting that amount from the assistance check, whether or not the recipient actuallys receives such income.

4. Permit the use of a declaration form, filled out by the applicant, as a principal source of information about an individuals's eligibility with verification limited to what is reasonably necessary to assure that expenditures under the program will be legal.

5. Simplify instructions for computing both needs and resources, thus enabling much of the task of budget determination to be done by auxiliary staff and freeing trained workers for other essential duties.[48]

These guidelines reinforced the rights of the welfare recipient and affirmed his human dignity. They also mandated the providing of services based upon objective standards rather than upon subjective impressions.

At various points in this decade, controversy over welfare elicited very bitter comments from those who regarded welfare as a right. They challenged the basic principles of the welfare program on the basis that it did little "to strengthen the initiative and self-respect of the recipient." Instead it demeaned the client, requiring him to "expose" the intimate details of his life, after which the recipient was told that the only aid for which he would qualify was "the kind and amounts recognized by the all-wise people who draw up the official budget."[49]

In addition, concern was expressed for those in most need who were frequently unable or unwilling to risk speaking out in criticism of the welfare system lest they be made to suffer added deprivation. As one writer expressed it:

> They are indeed vulnerable to human indignities and the impending if not already existing loss of their privileges and rights as American citizens. Theirs is a tenuous hold on those rights.[50]

The proponents of the right to public assistance recognized some of the problems related to their position. They spoke in terms of this being a right "with reciprocal obligation," or as a "contingent right," dependent upon the laws remaining in force and upon sufficient financial appropriations to maintain the programs.[51]

Progress toward universal recognition and acceptance of these rights was not characterized by steady growth. Frequently clients were forced to seek recourse and redress through the courts. In 1963, for instance, the American Civil Liberties Union intervened on behalf of Joseph LaFountain in a second welfare crisis. LaFountain and four others had been jailed in upper New York for allegedly refusing to work on a work-relief project. This confinement was viewed as a severe violation of LaFountain's basic civil rights and the antithesis of the democratic foundations of our society. As Betty Mandell reported in *Social Work:*

> The case of these five men was unprecedented in the recent history of this country, for although the state legally claims the right to force its citizens to work as punishment for a crime, it has never before claimed the right to force its free citizens to work under threat of being jailed.[52]

In brief, LaFountain and the others were assigned to a work-relief project by the County Welfare Department as part of the local requirements for receiving public assistance. The five men had worked for several months cutting brush, cleaning up the cemeteries, and building shoulders on new roads. In January 1963, they had been cutting back brush within twenty-five feet of an unpaved road. According to the foreman "the snow was up to your knees, and some of it was above your knees." Although the temperature was twelve or fifteen degrees above zero, the men had not been provided with adequate cold-weather clothing. They had been going home every night, soaked to the skin from the snow.[53]

On the morning of 30 January, when the foreman arrived, the men said that they were willing to do any other work, but they would not cut brush because the snow was too deep. They were even willing to cut brush next to the road in the same area, to sand roads, or to do any reasonable assignment. No one listened. Instead, on 1 February, affidavits were filed at the instigation of the County Welfare Director who intended to seek the "quick prosecution of welfare clients who did not cooperate with him."[54] This action resulted in the removal of the families of these men from Temporary Aid to Dependent Children Relief. They were transferred instead to Home Relief on the grounds that the refusal of the men to work made them ineligible for TADC grants. This move was criticized as being political and prejudicial. As Mandell observed:

> Actually, the change was made in an attempt to prove that the men's "refusal to work" increased the cost of their support to St. Lawrence County. . . . Rather the increase in cost was owing to the welfare department's juggling of categories in an attempt to build a case against the men. The men were not notified of this change . . . although this is legally required.[55]

The men were indicted, tried, and found guilty. LaFountain was sentenced to eight months in jail, the others to four months. The American Civil Liberties Union appealed the decision on the grounds that the imprisonment was in violation of the Thirteenth Amendment, the Antipeonage Act, and the due process clause of the Fourteenth Amendment. The Appellate Division of the Supreme Court of New York State supported the ACLU petition by reversing the conviction, thereby further clarifying the rights of welfare recipients.[56]

In a third court ruling, the right to legal services were extended to the poor. The United States Supreme Court in *Gideon* v. *Wainwright* held that the Fourteenth Amendment "makes provision for a fair trial obligatory on the states" and "reason and reflection require us to recognize that . . . any person hauled into court who is too poor to hire a lawyer cannot be assured a fair trial unless counsel is provided for him."[57]

The *Gault* decision of the Supreme Court also had tremendous impact upon the rights of welfare clients, children, and the mentally ill.[58] In this case, the Court affirmed the rights of the poor to an adequate notice of hearing, due process, a sufficient time for the preparation of a defense, the right of appeal, and the right to confront one's accusers. By inference, the client had the right to be evaluated by standards based upon fairness. The Court declared as unconstitutional the practice of many public welfare agencies of conducting midnight welfare raids, in entry and search of recipients' homes, and in threatening the loss of funds unless the recipient yielded to these tactics.[59]

Other court cases during this decade declared as unconstitutional the use of polygraphs by welfare agencies in determining paternity for prosecution, in the taking of punitive action against families with illegitimate children, and the use of residency requirements as a determination of eligibility for public assistance.[60]

As clients become more conscious of their rights and were better able to articulate their complaints, agencies repeatedly found their policies and practices scrutinized and sharply criticized by the courts. For instance, abuses were found in the treatment accorded the unmarried parent, with many reported incidents of pressured sterilization, withdrawal of payments, and compulsory criminal action against the alleged father.[61]

Another effort at clarifying clients' rights occurred in 1966 when Secretary of Health, Education and Welfare John Gardner issued a policy statement restraining welfare departments from using pressure to compel the use of birth control methods. By policy definition, the right of the client for self-determination was reaffirmed.[62]

Throughout the sixties, civil rights were interwoven with the right of the client to make his own decisions, to be self-determining. This, however, posed another value conflict for it raised the complicated issue of harmonizing the right to public assistance with the work ethic. Fear was expressed that recipients of welfare would lose the incentive to work, that they could refuse jobs for which they were competent and still continue to receive welfare funds, and that some welfare recipients might receive more money than low paid workers.

The influence of the work ethic can be seen by closely examining what was called the Nixon Welfare Plan presented as HR 14174 in the 1969 session of the 91st Congress. The plan as introduced contained several restrictive provisions.

a. Any person found eligible for welfare will be required to register with the local state employment office.

b. If a person fails to register, his portion of the family welfare will be canceled, "thereby reducing the income of an already needy family" and penalizing all family members for the actions of one.

c. If the person failing to register is the only adult member of a family, no welfare grant will at all come to that family until the responsible adult registers. In such cases, the secretary of health, education and welfare "may, if he deems it appropriate" (make provision) for payment . . . benefits . . . to any person, other than a member of such family who is interested in the welfare of the family.[63]

Many initial reactions to the proposed legislation noted that it appeared to be regressive. As David Gil observed:

A society which honestly aspires to social justice, and is serious about eliminating poverty and its disastrous concomitants, must be willing to institute a resource distribution system designed to maximize societal responsibility for the well-being, development, and self-realization of all its citizens, in place of a distribution system designed to maximize individual profit and economic self-interest.[64]

Almost as a countering force to the Nixon position, clients became more aware of their rights. They saw the need to join together and to become politically vocal. As Barbara Jordan lamented:

The poor have been X-rayed, dissected, examined, probed, accused, belittled, isolated, and brutalized. We have done everything to them except give them their humanity. Their plight is an indictment of every American whose stomach is full. We try to hide the poor under the freeways and behind billboards and bury them in bureaucratic red tape, but their presence cannot be denied. They are developing vocal and articulate spokesmen, and the poor will heard.

What will be their forum?[65]

It seemed as if the clients had to organize their own revolution in order to actualize the profession's commitment to client self-determination. Their efforts were not universally welcomed. Such clients and client groups were labeled as troublesome, disruptive, and agitative. They struggled to implement what the social work profession held in theory: (1) the right to cash grants; (2) the right to eligibility based upon equitable and objective standards; (3) the right to due process, including the right to notification and the right to appeal; (4) the right to representation by counsel when unable to pay for one; (5) the right to freedom of choice in family planning with corresponding rights of freedom from coercion, threat, or force; (6) the right to services; and (7) the right to freedom of movement.

These rights were seen as needing legal safeguards for there were violations of them, especially among rural populations and minority groups.[66] Obviously it was easier to discuss these rights in theory than it was to insure their implementation.

3. *The Right of Dissent.* If we were to view client self-determination as being on a continuum, at the one extreme would be little or no opportunity for the client to exercise his right of self-determination, and at the other end would be the opportunity for the client to be totally self-determining.

The events of the sixties, especially civil disobedience, appeared to move many towards the latter end of the continuum. While the Constitution guaranteed equality under the law as one of the deepest political principles of this society, the presence of segregation and discrimination and the use of illegal procedures by the government seriously challenged that concept. Civil disobedience seemed to highlight the need to distinguish between the *invasion* of rights on the one hand and the *preservation* of those rights on the other.[67] The problem remained in answering the question of how to bring about those necessary changes so that social justice might become a reality. To many this seemed to be the impossible dream.

Civil disobedience appeared to be a reasonable and a justifiable action. Given an inequitable state of affairs and a government that did not or would not effectively hear the concerns of the people, what nonviolent options were available? Civil disobedience appeared to be a civilized stratagem which had many precedents in great events in history. The Magna Carta and the Declaration of Independence were products of it. Some modern nations, for example India and several African nations, employed civil disobedience to gain political self-determination.

> . . . the time has been called "revolutionary," but in each case the revolution is a reaffirmation of ancient ideals . . . a surge of building upon old premises . . . a time of constitutional rehabilitation . . . . It is finally man's escape from the darkness of tyranny. It is the flowering of democracy.[68]

By seeking to establish social justice, the democratic way of life is brought much closer to reality, and civil disobedience becomes another dimension of the individual exercising his right of self-determination.

As was true in the fifties, writers in this decade continued to stress the need for extending self-determination to most, if not all, client populations. The presence of a handicap or a given condition or the stage of one's life were not sufficient reasons for denying or withholding the right of self-determination.

The worker was held responsible for understanding the client's needs and for using sound professional judgment and skills. He was cautioned to exercise his authority wisely and to provide opportunities for the client to increase his capabilities in these areas. Self-determination was considered an essential right of all clients and a crucial element of the social work relationship.

As new practice models were introduced and existing ones were extended, self-determination continued to be refined. This was particularly the case with social group work, with the development of social role theory as a practice model, and in the application of behavioral modification techniques to social work. As the profession began to shift from intervention at the individual level to intervention at the societal level, a review of self-determination seemed mandatory, especially in discussing social policy planning, social action, and advocacy.

4. *Social Group Work and Self-Determination.* During the sixties the use of the group method assumed increased importance as one of the major social work methods. Theoreticians and practitioners stressed the right of the client to be self-determining. Client self-determination continued as a key factor in evaluating the success of the group work method.

In working with groups, the social worker was responsible for creating the helping environment. This enabled the client to develop his capacities and potentialities for self-determination while maintaining restraint in the worker's use of authority.

Vinik portrayed the group worker as using the relationship "to give acceptance and support, to help clarify goals and means for their realization, and to help develop responsibility and individual self-determination."[69]

5. *Role Theory.* Social role theory was a major new contribution to the knowledge bank of social work. It focused on the

significance of roles and role expectations, role fulfillment and the perceptions of others.[70] Social roles were defined as

... what a person in a given social position and situation is expected to be, to act like, and to feel like and what the other(s) in relation to him are expected to be, to act like, and to feel like.[71]

A number of basic assumptions were postulated for using role theory in social work practice:

• Roles imply that certain activities and behaviors are required of any given status.

• Roles imply interaction of the individual with others; individual and individual, individual and group, individual and community.

• Roles imply that there are "social expectations" and social norms which serve as guides in regulating the interaction.

• Roles are interactional products of individual personality structure and individual processes on the one hand and the effect of group structure and group processes on the other.

• Healthy functioning is expressed through the performance of social roles.

• Roles imply that value statements are interjected in the interactional process.[72]

The interrelatedness of role theory with the principle of client self-determination was quickly recognized.

The caseworker will need first to learn from the client what his ideas of the role norms are (as well as what he has invested in them emotionally). He will need to match those conceptions of norms against the range of what is given acceptance or sanction in the community. He may need to help his client come to accept different norms, or to help his clients, two or more, develop compromises among their standards for themselves and for one another.[73]

The caseworker who starts from what his client sees and wants, and who works to bring that client into more harmonious relationship with what others require or expect, will not readily "impose" his values, "middleclass" or other.[74]

6. *Self-Determination and Behavioral Modification.* Behavior modification was another theoretical approach developed during this decade. It stimulated much controversy, particularly in relationship to the principle of client self-determination. Edwin J. Thomas enumerated the following assumptions as "common to all behavioral modification techniques":

• Behavioral approaches emphasize the learned aspects of behavior.

• There is a focus upon observable responses.

• Treatment consists of achieving behavioral maintenance or modification.

• The objectives of behavioral intervention are the acquisition, strengthening, maintenance, weakening, or elimination of behavior.

• Strong emphasis is given to contemporary conditions which may serve to sustain or reinforce existing behavior.[75]

The behavioral model, like other social work models, claims to be based upon an assessment of the behaviors which "define the problem for the client." During the assessment phase the social worker observes the client's behavior noting those events which precede the disturbing behavior and the consequences of that behavior. Through this evaluation a behavioral modification program is proposed. It may use operant-related techniques, respondent-related techniques, or some combination of them. Operant techniques are those which focus upon behavioral outcomes or that behavior which is "voluntary and governed by its consequences." The six operant techniques commonly identified include positive reinforcement, extinction, differential reinforcement, response-shaping, negative reinforcement, and punishment.[76]

The use of the operant-conditioning techniques, especially punishment, aroused much concern within the profession. Thomas maintained that punishment was already being utilized by many social workers, disguised under euphemistic labels such as "worker's expression of disapproval," the withdrawal of privileges, "setting limits," and the "use of authority."[77] Thomas contended that punishment is a purposefully directed response of the social worker, based upon his study and diagnosis of the client's situation.

The behavioral model was accused of being "manipulative," "robotistic," "atomistic," and "unethical."[78] These charges primarily related to how the worker used his authority and to the principle of client self-determination. It serves our purposes here to see how the profession responded to these charges. Several writers, arguing in support of the behavioral model, felt that the charges were based on either a lack of understanding of the model or a misinterpretation of the language. The behavioral approach, they maintained, was represented in all the therapies concerned with bringing about behavioral change. The client comes or is brought to the worker because his behavior is disturbing to someone. This model still upholds the need for the client's cooperation and for the social worker to respect the dignity and worth of the client.

As to the specific charges leveled against the behavioral approach, Aronowitz and Weinberg responded to the criticism of robotism:

> This is the portrayal of the behaviorally oriented therapist, the person who advocates the application of learning theory to treatment of the individual or who insists on systematically applying psychological science to societal problems, as one who is cold, impersonal, and mechanical in his approach, as a destroyer of freedom, an enemy of love, a little un-American, and ultimately a menace to society. The picture is of a mechanical robot who advocates the control and manipulation of behavior as a good thing in itself. . . . Herein probably lies the heart of the difference of view. What (Rollo) May says a behaviorist is advocating, the behaviorist argues actually exists, namely that psychotherapy is an influence process. To deny it is to hide from one's real responsibilities. It is neither good nor bad, it is the therapy process.[79]

As to the behavioral model being atomistic or too limited, focusing on only a single stimulus or set of responses instead of dealing with the whole person in his total environment, the reply is a denial of the charges. The defense argues that focusing upon a single stimulus is identical with "partialization of the problem," a technique respected and widely used by the profession. Each part-symptom or stimulus is viewed as being interrelated with the totality of the individual's behavior and not simply as an isolated event. Rather than being too limited, the behavioral approach claimed to be highly individualized.[80]

The charge that the behavioral model was unethical and manipulative drew a response from Thomas and from others. He noted that any new theory must, as part of the process of establishing itself, answer the charge of being unethical. All knowledge, he maintained, possesses the potential of being used for either good or evil. The ethical consideration pertains to the purpose or intent of the worker, the goals of the client, and the manner of application. "Knowledge itself is ethically neutral."[81]

Murrow and Gochras also responded to this accusation by arguing that there was "pervasive use of social influence and indoctrination" in all models of social work practice regardless of "protestations to the contrary."[82] Bruck contended that the "active orientation" of the behaviorist "leads him to exercise much greater influence and control over the conduct of the treatment . . . than does the more nondirective, traditional practitioner."[83]

Murrow and Gochras contended that while the role of the behavioral therapist is a very active one, it still qualified as a "therapist-client" partnership.[84]

Practitioners of the behavioral model insisted that the right of the client to make his own choice is a critical, integral feature of this approach. Moreover, as in any mutually agreed upon contract, there are responsibilities and obligations on both sides of the contract relationship.

To the issue of control, Bandura countered by observing that behavior is controlled; the issue is not one of imposing control where none existed before, but rather substituting new controlling conditions for those that have regulated a person's behavior.

A person is considered free insofar as he can partly influence future events by managing his own behavior . . . . The self-control process begins by informing individuals of the types of behaviors they will have to practice to produce desired outcomes, or ways in which they can institute stimuli to increase the occurrence of requisite performances, and of how they can arrange self-reinforcing consequences to sustain them.[85]

Bandura summed up the attitude of behaviorists:

Behavioral change procedures that involve role enactment also depend upon the self-determination of outcomes through clients' regulation of their own behavior and the environmental contingencies that reciprocally influence it. Contrary to common belief, behavioral approaches not only can support a humanistic morality, but because of their relative effectiveness in establishing self-determination these methods hold much greater promise than traditional procedures for enhancement of behavioral freedom and fulfillment of human capabilities.[86]

In summary, the *theory* of client self-determination was again reevaluated, this time in a very turbulent period in the life of the nation. There was a heightened sensitivity to the legal rights of persons in the lower socioeconomic strata. And with the vigorous championing of the rights of the underprivileged, there was a surprising and unexpected emphasis upon the concept of client responsibility. The mutuality and interdependence of rights and duties were recognized for the first time with clarity and strength. Prior to this the stress was almost exclusively upon rights.

A number of value issues inherent in self-determination were noted, and a theoretical correlation with existential philosophy was briefly explored. Each of the three major conferences included a substantial consideration of some of the value themes associated with client self-determination, such as: individual freedom and social responsibility; interdependence of man and society; value priorities and conflicts; the international applicability of self-determination; and the relationship of self-determination to social welfare and social justice.

The *practice* of client self-determination was advanced by legal means, by court decisions concerning the rights of clients to public assistance, which eventually resulted in the 1962 amendments to public welfare. Civil disobedience, based on the right to dissent, was another suggested way to secure social justice.

The introduction of the behavior modification model of psychosocial therapy caused a mild furor in this decade. The central issue of the debate was whether or not the methodology of this particular model contained a violation of the principle of client self-determination.

ENDNOTES FOR CHAPTER 6

1   White House Chief of Staff, John Ehrlichman, spokesman for President Nixon, castigated social workers as "parasites living off the fiscal policy" and admonished them to seek honest work.

2   Helen Harris Perlman, "Social Work Method: A Review of the Past Decade," *Trends in Social Work Practice and Knowledge* (New York: National Association of Social Work, 1966), p. 80.

3   Virginia L. Tanner, "The Public Welfare Worker in Family Crisis," *The Social Welfare Forum: 1962* (New York: Columbia University Press, 1962), p. 203.

4   Robert Morris, "New Concepts in Community Organization," *The Social Welfare Forum: 1961* (New York: Columbia University Press, 1961), p. 128.

5   For example, see: Scott Briar and Henry Miller, *Problems and Issues in Social Casework* (New York: Columbia University Press, 1971), p. 40; Edmund Arthur Smith, *Social Welfare: Principles and Concepts* (New York: Association Press, 1965), pp. 22-23; Florence Hollis, *Casework: A Psycho-Social Therapy* (New York: Random House, 1964), p. 12.

6   Ernest Greenwood, "Attributes of the Profession," *Social Work*, July 1957, pp. 44-45; Saul Bernstein, "Self-Determination: King or Citizen in the Realm of Values," *Social Work*, January 1960, pp. 3-8.

7   Mary Gyarfas, "Social Science, Technology, and Social Work: A Caseworker's View," *Social Service Review*, September 1969, p. 263.

8   Greenwood, "Attributes of the Profession," p. 48.

9   Helen Harris Perlman, "Self-Determination: Reality or Illusion?," *Social Service Review*, December 1965, p. 420.

10   Briar and Millar, *Problems and Issues in Social Casework*, pp. 42-44.

11 Alan Keith-Lucas, "A Critique of the Principle of Self-Determination," *Social Work*, July 1963, p. 67.

12 Ibid., p. 71.

13 David Soyer, "The Right to Fail," *Social Work*, July 1963, p. 77.

14 Ibid., p. 78.

15 John J. Stretch, "Existentialism: A Proposed Philosophical Orientation for Social Work," *Social Work*, October 1967; Donald F. Krill, "Existential Psychotherapy and the Problem of Anomie," *Social Work*, April 1969; Donald F. Krill "Existentialism: A Philosophy for Our Current Revolutions," *Social Service Review*, September 1966.

16 Frank Thilly and Leogea Wood, *A History of Philosophy* (New York: Henry Holt and Company, 1955), p. 579; Stretch, "Existentialism," p. 98.

17 Krill, "Existential Psychotherapy," p. 41.

18 Ibid., p. 42.

19 Felix P. Biestek, "Basic Values in Social Work," *Values in Social Work: A Re-Examination* (New York: National Association of Social Work, 1967), pp. 11-12.

20 Felix P. Biestek, "Problems in Identifying Values," *Values in Social Work: A Re-Examination* (New York: National Association of Social Work, 1967), pp. 23 ff.

21 Charles G. Chakerian, "Variations in Values," *Values in Social Work: A Re-Examination* (New York: National Association of Social Work, 1967), p. 38.

22 Ibid.

23 Helen Harris Perlman, "Self-Determination: Reality or Illusion?," *Values in Social Work: A Re-Examination* (New York: National Association of Social Work, 1967), p. 52.

24 Ibid.

25 Ibid., pp. 65-66.

26 Saul Bernstein, "Conflict, Self-Determination, and Social Work," *Values in Social Work: A Re-Examination* (New York: National Association of Social Work, 1967), pp. 75-77.

27 Alan Keith-Lucas, "Self-Determination and the Changing Role of the Social Worker," *Values in Social Work: A Re-Examination* (New York: National Association of Social Work, 1967), pp. 84 ff.

28 Martin Teicher, "Conclusion and Summary," *Values in Social Work: A Re-Examination* (New York: National Association of Social Work, 1967), p. 107.

29 Council on Social Work Education and Intercultural Exploration, *Universals and Difference in Social Work Values, Functions, and Practice* (New York: Council on Social Work Education, 1967), p. 5.

30 Ibid., p. 11.

31 Ibid., p. 23.

32 Ibid., p. 25.
33 Ibid., p. 72.
34 John B. Turner, "Report of the Pre-Conference Working Party," *Social Welfare and Human Rights* (New York: Columbia University Press, 1969), pp. 3-4.
35 Ibid., pp. 4-5.
36 Ibid., pp. 6-7.
37 Ibid., pp. 8-9.
38 Ibid., p. 14.
39 Andre Franco Montoro, "The Universal Declaration of Human Rights," *Social Welfare and Human Rights* (New York: Columbia University Press, 1969), p. 44.
40 Ibid., p. 46.
41 Dieter Hanart, "The Rights of the Client," *Social Welfare and Human Rights* (New York: Columbia University Press, 1969), p. 153.
42 Alan Reitman, "Civil Rights and Civil Liberties in the 1960's," *Encyclopedia of Social Work*, 15th ed. (New York: National Association of Social Workers, 1965), p. 160.
43 "Notes and Comments," *Social Service Review*, September 1961, p. 310.
44 Ibid.
45 Ibid.
46 Ibid., pp. 310-311.
47 Editorial, "The Dark Ages in Newburgh?," *New York Times*, June 29, 1961.
48 Ellen Winston, "The Contribution of Social Welfare to Economic Growth," *The Social Welfare Forum: 1966* (New York: Columbia University Press, 1966), pp. 16-17.
49 Eveline M. Burns, "What's Wrong with Public Welfare?," *Social Service Review*, June 1962, pp. 113-114.
50 Lloyd Setleis, "Civil Rights and the Rehabilitation of AFDC Clients," *Social Work*, April 1964, p. 4.
51 Burns, "What's Wrong with Public Welfare?," p. 120; Hasseltine Byrd Taylor, "The Nature of the Right to Public Assistance," *Social Service Review*, September 1962, p. 267.
52 Betty Mandell, "The Crime of Poverty," *Social Work*, January 1966, p. 11.
53 Ibid.
54 Ibid., p. 12.
55 Ibid., p. 13.
56 Ibid.
57 *Gideon* v. *Wainwright*, 372 U.S. 335-352 (1963).
58 *In re Gault*, 387 U.S. 1 (1967).
59 B. James George, Jr., *Gault and the Juvenile Court Revolution* (Ann

Arbor, Michigan: Institute of Continuing Legal Education, 1968), p. 79 ff

60 Ibid., pp. 89-91.

61 Vera Shlakman, "Unmarried Parenthood: An Approach to Social Policy," *Social Casework*, October 1966, p. 494 ff.

62 John Garner, "Family Planning and Population Programs," Statement or the Department of Health, Education and Welfare, January 1966.

63 HR 14174, 91st Congress, 1st Session, 1969, pp. 17-19.

64 David G. Gil, "Mother's Wages—An Alternative Attack on Poverty," *Social Work Practice: 1969* (New York: Columbia University Press, 1969), p. 189.

65 Barbara Jordan, "Income Security Policies—The Heineman Commission Proposal," *The Social Welfare Forum: 1970* (New York: Columbia University Press, 1970), p. 25.

66 See: Setleis, "Civil Rights," p. 8; George, *Gault and the Juvenile Court Revolutions*, pp. 98-106; Leon Ginsberg, "Social Problems in Rural America," *Social Work Practice: 1969* (New York: Columbia University Press, 1969), pp. 180-81.

67 Mary L. Hemmy, "Protective Services for Older People," *Social Work Practice: 1963* (New York: Columbia University Press, 1963), p. 119.

68 Sol Morton Isaac, "Law and Social Welfare," *The Social Welfare Forum: 1965* (New York: Columbia University Press, 1965), p. 6.

69 Abe Vinik, "Role of the Group Service Agency," *Social Work*, July 1964, p. 103.

70 For a fuller explanation of social role theory, see Helen Harris Perlman, *Persona: Social Role and Responsibility* (Chicago: University of Chicago Press, 1968).

71 Helen Harris Perlman, "The Role Concept and Social Casework: Some Explorations," *Social Service Review*, December 1961, p. 374.

72 Ibid., pp. 376-77; Paul Glasser, "Social Role, Personality and Group Work," *Social Work Practice: 1962* (New York: Columbia University Press, 1962), pp. 63-65.

73 Perlman, "The Role Concept and Social Casework," p. 377.

74 Ibid., p. 378.

75 Edwin J. Thomas, "The Behavioral Modification Approach," *Encyclopedia of Social Work*, 16th ed. (New York: National Association of Social Workers, 1971), pp. 1226-227.

76 Edwin J. Thomas, "Selected Sociobehavioral Techniques and Principles: An Approach to Interpersonal Helping," *Social Work*, January 1968, p. 16.

77 Ibid., pp. 22-23.

78 Eugene Aronowitz and Denise Weinberg, "The Utilization of Reinforcement Theory in Social Group Work," *Social Service Review*, December 1966, pp. 390-93.

79 Leonard Krasner, "The Behavioral Scientist and Social Responsibility: No Place to Hide," cited in Aronowitz and Weinberg, "Utilization of Reinforcement Theory," pp. 390-91.
80 William Murrow and Harvey L. Gochras, "Misconceptions Regarding Behavioral Modification," *Social Service Review*, September 1970, pp. 300-01.
81 Thomas, "Sociobehavioral Techniques," p. 25.
82 Murrow and Gochras, "Misconceptions," pp. 301-02.
83 Max Bruck, "Behavior Modification Theory and Practice: A Critical Review," *Social Work*, April 1968, p. 45.
84 Murrow and Gochras, "Misconceptions," p. 302.
85 Albert Bandura, *Principles of Behavior Modification* (New York: Holt, Rinehart and Winston, 1969), p. 88.
86 Ibid.

Intervention at the societal level_____
_____ Social planning_____ Social action
_____ Advocacy _____

CHAPTER 7

1960—1969 PART II

THE TURBULENT events of the sixties, including the civil rights movement, the struggle with massive urban and rural problems, and the unresolved plight of those caught in poverty, caused social work to be redirected from a concern which focused primarily upon the individual to intervention at the societal level.

INTERVENTION AT THE SOCIETAL LEVEL

During this period, the call was for *social* work to return to its historical social orientation, for the profession to recruit new leadership committed to dealing with broader social issues, and to become involved in social planning and social action. Social

159

workers were characterized as divided into three camps: those who retained the "clinical" orientation of social work; those who maintained the need for a "social" orientation and the use of political and social action as acceptable techniques; and those who urged a combined, dual focus for the profession.[1]

The clinical orientation was directed to the treatment of the individual and the improvement of his social functioning; the social orientation was primarily directed to changing unjust social structures which impeded the healthy functioning of many in American society. Frequently these were cast as being opposites.[2]

These challenges prompted much serious thought. Kahn, for instance, proposed that social work ought to restrict itself as the "primary discipline of a social planning state."[3] Feldman and Specht suggested dividing the focus of social work into "micro-problems" and "macro-problems."[4]

Traditionally, a dichotomy was made between behavioral models. One model focused upon psychopathology and the restructuring of the human personality. The other, a "social systems" model, stressed the effect upon man of socially determined forces. Wade felt that a synthesis of both models was needed.[5]

Scott Briar welcomed this changing focus because, although the clinical approach had been beneficial for many, it served far too few and frequently too late.[6]

Garvin and Glasser proposed "social treatment" as a new model for the profession, bringing together a number of interventive techniques. By doing so, "the helping process would then fit the client, rather than the client fit the method." In this framework social treatment would focus upon the problems and the needs of both the individual and the community. While the therapeuic objectives of personality growth and change remained central, they were also seen to be "inextricably bound up by social structure, social change, and community institutions."[7]

Meyer, responding from a somewhat different perspective, observed that in the history of social work there have been five practice models which have been of value to the profession. The first method involved a degree of passivity on the part of the social worker: the client acted upon his own situation while the social worker waited for him to do his own changing. The second model reflected on an educational approach, with the social worker providing for the client:

> . . . all of the then conceived opportunities for change or modification of behavior and situation whether the technical emphasis was upon the relationship, support, advice, relief, or other services, change was to come about through the strengthening of the client by casework actions, so that he would be more capable of dealing with his life.[8]

The third model was the medical or clinical one, with social workers becoming preoccupied with "cure" and personality changes and with changing pathologic and maladjusted behaviors.

The fourth model, of more recent experience, was the political model:

> . . . where the client has been pressed into service on his own behalf and has been expected to change his own condition through social action, lobbying, striking, or exerting pressure upon power groups. This model has avoided recognition of individual needs and pathology in its emphasis upon social change to be effected by, as well as for, the client groups.[9]

In the fifth or "public health model," the client's problems are not only to be viewed individually and personally but they almost must be understood in the broader framework of the "societal and epidemiological forces that contribute to his (the client's) lifestyle as well as to his problems."[10]

These five models are part of the open system of social work, a system which has been responsive to the changing demands of society and to the needs of its people.

These models demonstrate the variation of themes of social concern over the years. As the focus changed, so did the role of the worker; new demands were also made upon the government. No longer could a governmental "hands-off policy" be tolerated.

It was not just for the sake of the needy, but rather for the welfare of the whole society. No longer could poverty be simply endured without understanding the serious, detrimental effects it had upon the whole fabric of society.

To seek changes at the societal level would enable the profession to attain its long desired goals of "restoration, provision, and prevention."[11] These changes would be necessary prerequisites for individual self-fulfillment, self-realization, and self-determination. With man and society interdependent, change needed to be directed towards both so that man and society might be able to achieve their potential.

Acceptance of this point of view was not universally welcomed by the professional community nor by the general public. Wade commented that the profession had struggled before with two very divergent definitions of social work. The first definition viewed interventive action in terms of the goals of social adjustment, "not adjustment at any price, but certainly adjustment as defined and limited by the structure of an agency." He criticized this definition in that it sought to maintain the "social status quo" and would not bring about any basic changes or relieve any problems. Therefore, "a profession primarily guided either explicitly or implicitly by this definition will not be meeting the many needs that arise in a rapidly changing society."[12]

The second definition, he suggested, focused upon consciously directed change and was guided by the worker's personal commitment to the philosophical ideals and values of the profession. It was not limited by the function and purpose of the agency.

> Social work practice is the conscious application of behavioral science knowledge toward the goal of effecting planned change in individuals, groups, and social systems. Action directed toward such change is guided by the values, methods, and techniques acknowledged by, and identified with, the social work profession.[13]

Wade called for directing professional efforts towards the political system, using the legislative powers of government to insure positive, effective societal change for the welfare of all.[14]

During this decade and related to this discussion, self-determination was expressed as the right of the client to participate in program development, policy determination, distribution of local funds, and in the establishment of priorities.

SOCIAL PLANNING

Social policy, as defined within the social work frame of reference, includes "the principles and procedures guiding any measure or course of action dealing with individual and aggregate relationship in society." It also is conceived as "intervention in and regulation of an otherwise random social system" and represents a course of action which "governs social relationships and distribution of resources within a society."[15]

Social planning is the process by which "the formulation of policies to reduce social problems and the execution of action that achieve the desired results came about."[16]

Planning, as a process, includes a basic set of functions required for problem solving:

1. Intelligence gathering, information analysis, problem definition.

2. Structure building, including development of relationships, channels of communication, and organization among the participants.

3. Policy formulation, including the selection of goals, alternative goals, and strategy development translated into a plan of action.

4. Plan implementation.[17]

Boehm proposed five areas of concern as the proper focus of social planning: need identification; resource coordination; resource creation; resource delivery; and resource utilization.[18] These serve to identify the nature of the social change being sought. By means of the planning process, strategies could be developed to bring about the desired changes. Once the plan is moved into the action phase, evaluation and possible reformulation or refinement of the goals would be part of the ongoing process.

An essential component of the planning process, especially in the determination of priorities, is citizen participation. The desirable *degree* of participation seemed to remain the issue. Participation could appear to extend from full involvement of the people in social planning to mere token representation. For instance, Titmuss and Jolander cautioned against "overestimating the potentialities of the poor" and urged proceeding very cautiously because "they (the poor) aren't ready."[19]

Sometimes, in spite of strenuous opposition, citizen participation in social planning was identified among the four "basic social goals" of the modern individual goals which included a sense of welfare, justice, achievement, and participation.[20]

The authority for this participation is an extension of the meaning of the words found in the preamble to the Constitution. Here "We, the People" assumes new meaning as previously disenfranchised people, especially the minorities and the poor, claimed their rights and responsibilities as citizens. One of the basic rights demanded was the right of self-determination, to have the freedom of choice for the future—their own future and that of their children. This sense of participation was described as the very meaning of a democratic way of life.

If this right was not implemented, the people would find new mechanisms, new ways to deal with problems, both good and evil ways. By the end of this decade, the voices of the people could be heard across the country, demanding their right to choose. This chorus, born out of hope and frustration, was the result of a decade which had experienced protests and marches, legal blockades and legal victories. Some campaigned for federal legislation and thus achieved "maximum feasible participation"; others sought governmental policy change which would implement this legislation. The movement to gain increased citizen participation was described as "the very lifeblood of our democracy."[21] Social workers were called to use authority constructively, especially when dealing with community power structures. Unless these sources of power were mobilized, no positive institutional change would be possible.

> If strong social work leadership is not there with ideas, directives and authority to make its contribution, the community will find leadership elsewhere.

> Our whole society has attained such a level of institutional and bureaucratic development as to demand a reconsideration of the new perspective in which the individual finds himself. For the individual in modern society attains and maintains his importance in and through institutional life. Social institutions, of which community planning is one, have new meaning even for the highly personalized aspects of the individual, such as rights, and freedom, and self-determination. Individual freedom is greatly dependent upon and draws its practical meaning from institutional strength and institutional freedom.[22]

Where "citizen" in citizen participation had been used in Plato's terms as "one of the elite or one held fit to govern," it was now interpreted to mean "those who are assumed to be the beneficiaries of service . . . . potential 'indigenous leaders'."[23] This was a very significant change of direction. The principle of client self-determination would no longer be a hollow philosophical concept; it had the potential of being a real power base of operation. This would not be a simple task, as Hayden observed:

> Self-determination cannot be "granted." It is always wrestled from those who oppose it. People first win self-determination, then their former oppressors "grant" it . . . . The battle for self-determination is long or short, peaceful or bloody, according to the degree of vested interest and determination of the oppressed.[24]

Now self-determination was both the end and the means for attaining the goal of personal freedom. The planning phase was quite clear, direct, and pertinent, but the question of its feasibility remained. This could be answered only by effective social action.

SOCIAL ACTION

Social action was defined as action which "encompasses individual or group activity designated to influence a change in social policy." Social action represents "part of the birthright of each human being: his responsibility and privilege to attempt to mold the environment in terms of his values."[25] Social action contains two dimensions, one significant for the client, the other as a focus for the worker. For the client, it includes direct participation and activity in those matters which affect his daily living. For the worker, social action is a method of intervention "to bring about social change," involving a series of interventive actions and strategies "directed rationally towards preconceived goals."[26]

A variety of rural and urban community action programs came into being in this decade. These programs served three main purposes:

1. To obtain participation of clients, both actual and potential, in services designed to overcome their disabilities.

2. To gain the participation of the disadvantaged and functionally disenfranchised groups in the body politic.

3. To use community participation as therapy through which individuals and groups could gain confidence, self-esteem, and a sense of power which would make it possible for them to obtain and utilize opportunities available through the institutions of society from which they are now alienated.[27]

This welding together of self-determination and political power was directed towards reaching, teaching, and strengthening the sequence of the perceived and/or real denial of access to participation on the various local boards created under the "maximum feasible participation" clause of the 1964 antipoverty legislation.[28]

The primary objectives for citizen participation in those federal programs were to decrease alienation, to engage the "sick individual" in the process that will lead to his own healing, to create a neighborhood power group capable of influencing the distribution of resources, and to develop a base of support for a particular program.[29] Unless the disadvantaged were able to join forces and take collective political action to resolve their problems, nothing was likely to change.

Social workers were faced with the choice of becoming involved in political realities or of failing to fulfill their commitment. Many were reluctant to do the former. Yet the need for this type of intervention was real. Some agencies over the years had evolved into bureaucracies which now failed to serve the people for whose assistance they were created. To successfully confront such a system required the use of political power. To bring about change or to reform "implies influencing those who are empowered to make authoritative decisions and to obtain widespread public acceptance of reform measures."[30]

Community development and social action appeared to usher social work into an era of new programs and projects. The emphasis was upon freedom of choice, self-help, and self-determination.[31] Such programs as the Mississippi Project of the National Federation of Settlement Houses,[32] the Rankin County Assembly, another NFS project, and the Project ENABLE programs,[33] all served to reach out to the potential users of the services. By helping them to develop and secure those services for themselves, they had proved that they had the potential for independent action, for becoming more self-determining and for helping others to do so.

Another example of an innovative community program was the Mobilization for Youth project in New York City. This focused on juvenile delinquency prevention and control. It offered broad-scale services in the fields of employment, education, casework, group work, and community organization. Through its leadership, outreach efforts stimulated lower-income families to participate in efforts to resolve community problems. Their participation was a means of increasing their self-worth and developing a sense of community identification. As part of its role, Mobilization for Youth intervened in the social systems confronting their clients and often served as advocates for them. Consequently, the project encountered tremendous obstacles and great resistance.[34]

Among the revolutionary services developed by MFY was the establishment of legal services for the poor. By teaching the clients their rights and by providing back-up legal services, the poor were able to become more assertive of their rights. At times the use of the courts caused embarrassment and consternation, especially when the target of the suit happened to be another public or privately sponsored agency. The use of the courts, considered to be a valid technique in social action, was another extension and expression of the right to be self-determining.

Social action and self-determination assumed two other forms during this period. In one, it was the demand of the poor for control of various agencies and institutions in their community: for instance, community control over the public school system in the ghetto, the right to hire and fire staff, involvement in curriculum planning and policy decisions, and control over the planning and development of housing, parks, and recreational facilities in their communities. Such demands drew banner headlines in papers across the country. In some communities, these demands intensified the apprehension of the power structures.

> Whites cannot understand how the democratic concept of citizen participation got turned into demands for community control. And yet the white man who sends his children to private schools controls the educational policy boards . . . and the parents in the suburban communities control the destiny and education of their children. And the whites, who purchase Blue Cross policies and can hire their personal physicians, are in control of the health of their youngsters . . . . The white middle class is in control of its housing destiny. The black ghetto is not.[35]

The social work profession found the call for "community control" to have moved from being "out there" to being "right here" as demands were presented to the National Conference on Social Welfare in 1968, 1969, and 1970. A number of organizations formed a coalition and challenged the philosophy of the NCSW and the credibility of its leadership. This coalition was comprised of the National Welfare Rights Organization, the National Federation of Student Social Workers, the National Association of Black Social Workers, the United Native Americans, the Association of Puerto Rican Social Workers, and La Raza. Their collective complaint was brought to the conference floor by the chairperson of the National Welfare Rights Organization, Mrs. Johnnie Tellman.

> The heat is on. Black folks and poor white folks are not fighting any more. You can't make one believe that he's better than the other. Dr. Cohen made some very good points but he's been making them for a long time. He's had many articles and books published, and yet the system stays the same . . . . We want change and we will get it because we are not divided—we are together.[36]

The other form of self-determination through social action was the emergence of black unity groups. In part they represented a coming together of blacks, out of mutual concern, for the purpose of collective action. In some instances it brought with it the use of black power or a renewed interest in black nationalism as well as demands for control over the economy of the ghetto.

> The term "black unity" refers to a degree of consensus among blacks on issues, problems, and solutions facing the black community in America. The term "self-determination" refers to a willingness of black people to take action or actions to eradicate the problem of poverty and racism in American society.[37]

For social welfare to respond adequately to these demands, it would have to change its strategy from clinical treatment and rehabilitation to one which required involvement in broad intervention to improve human living conditions. This would include seeking changes in education, housing, health, justice, income maintenance, and community participation. The movement of the poor, the minorities, the disenfranchised seeking their identity, self-respect, and self-value through self-determination was a notable development—only history will be able to reveal the degree of its success.

ADVOCACY: THE CHANGING ROLE
OF THE SOCIAL WORKER

The rapid fire events of this decade, the spiraling problems of urban centers and the ever-increasing complexity of the needs of the people being served, called attention to the need for intervention in social systems via social planning and social action. Change was mandated from within the profession as well as from without, and the professional was required to assume new or modified professional roles.

> We (social workers) must become multipurpose in what we must think and act in terms of social policy and social action as well as social treatment. We must attack the basic problems of community attitudes. Every practitioner, every agency, needs to learn how to bring the facts of individual suffering, of community deterioration to the attention of opinion-makers and the general public. To get a hearing we may have to resort to dramatic, unorthodox methods. In any case, it will take courage. But the time is ripe, the climate propitious.[38]

Creative and innovative social workers were necessary in order to effect positive social change. This required professional reexamination of current methods and techniques and the development of new strategies and mechanisms of intervention. These would provide the client with more adequate opportunities for self-fulfillment.

The role of the social worker was portrayed in a number of diverse ways. But the central purpose remained consistent: to focus upon providing opportunities to increase the self-respect, self-confidence, and self-worth of the people being served. The basics of social work philosophy, namely the recognition of the innate dignity and worth of the individual, acceptance of him, and respect of his need and right to be self-determining, were reaffirmed. The social worker as a public servant was literally interpreted to mean just that—one who gives professional service, but who remains a servant.

Advocacy, when added to the description of the social worker's role, became the fulfillment of the worker's professional obligation to fight for his client's rights and needs. It embraced the principle of involving the client in the action, of helping the client in the action, and of helping the client to help himself in the area of social action as well.

During this decade, the role of the worker was broadened to include such functions as advocate, backbone builder, leader, teacher, lawyer, and occasionally that of enabler.[39] In other contexts the role was associated with an awesome array of responsibilities, including systems change agent, trouble-shooter,[40] social parent, group leader, community caretaker, social reformer, contact man, service specialist, coordinator, expediter, mediator, innovator, and guide-teacher.[41]

Kahn, in his definition, identified the role of the social worker as an advocate, helper, facilitator, enabler, and expert-consultant.[42] Others suggested that the social worker serve as a catalyst,[43] a social broker,[44] and/or an ombudsman.[45]

The role which seemed to stimulate the greatest amount of discussion was that of the advocate. There was sufficient professional concern to prompt the National Association of Social Workers to establish the Ad Hoc Committee on Advocacy in 1968. This committee wrestled with a number of problems including the definition of advocacy itself, its usefulness to the worker, problems related to advocacy and the use of authority, the legal model from which advocacy derived, professional responsibilities of the worker to client, community, and agency, and the problem of values conflict.

The Ad Hoc Committee defined advocacy in two ways:

1. one who pleads the cause of another, as in the legal advocate;

2. one who argues for, defends, maintains or recommends a cause or a proposal as in the political advocate.[46]

In professional literature, both definitions have been utilized.

a. The lawyer-advocate:

The caseworker was to be his client's supporter, his adviser, his champion, and, if need be, his representative in his dealings with the court, the police, the social agency, and other organizations . . . .[47]

b. The advocate-reformer:

> ... identifies with the plight of the disadvantaged ... tough-minded and partisan representation of their interests .... This role inevitably requires that the practitioner function as a political tactician.[48]

The Ad Hoc Committee noted that there was a similarity and an overlapping in both definitions and that there might be situations wherein the social worker would be called upon to perform within both definitions.[49]

One question raised during this discussion was related to whether it was possible for true advocacy to be in harmony with self-determination. As Kurzman and Solomon viewed the "advocacy dilemma," client self-determination here is difficult to implement because "the advocate generally determines the best course of action for the client's welfare. Advocate-determination rather than client-determination tends to establish a client dependency which is counter to the tradition and goals of social work."[50]

Client self-determination was also questioned on the grounds of the many constraints placed upon the advocate, including the goals and policies of the agency and the lack of necessary legal education and training.[51] Briar wondered whether the worker could represent both client and agency (the worker's employer).[52] The Ad Hoc Committee raised the possibility of value conflicts for the social worker, in that by promoting his client's interests, might he not be "injuring other aggrieved persons with an equally just claim?"[53]

One response offered to resolve some of the questions of the compatibility between advocacy and client self-determination:

> The advocate does not simply "take over"; he does not assume sole responsibility. Advocacy is a partnership relationship, to which the social worker brings professional knowledge and skill to help the client analyze his problem, identify the decisions that need to be made, elicit the client's choice among available options, and draft a plan for action. The client's active participation in each phase is solicited and expected ....

It should be emphasized that performance of the advocacy function to the point where the client has the experience of making his wishes felt and having them acted on can enhance, sometimes dramatically, his sense of confidence, competence, and mastery and reduce the feelings of apathy and impotence many of our clients experience in their dealings with the organizations that affect their lives.[54]

However, the social worker is not just a servant who must run to the client for an explicit approval for every contemplated action. Circumstances may demand that the advocate act independently because consultation with the client would not be feasible. In those instances the advocate realizes the special ethical responsibility he is assuming.

Through this role he is implicated in the lives of certain groups of people; thus his actions affect their lives directly for good or ill. Similarly, his work role gives him authority and influence over the lives of his clients; thus he has special ethical obligations regarding them.[55]

The question of client loyalty versus agency loyalty is not easily resolved. The social worker has responsibilities to both the client and the agency. The Committee attempted to resolve this dilemma by assuming the position that when the worker is performing the advocate role and gets into difficulty with his agency, that "NASW has an obligation to the worker that takes priority over its obligation to the agency. In effect, the worker is acting in behalf of the professional community."[56]

This position raises other serious value conflicts and is not without some dangers and risks, regardless of the choice that is made. The worker may well feel he is caught on the horns of the dilemma:

To whom, then, is the worker's primary responsibility: the agency or the client? If the former, the issue is simply met. If the latter— as in the case of the advocate—the agency may well become a target for a change.[57]

If indeed the worker feels he must be the one or the other, he can do no less than choose the client and be prepared to cast his lot with the enemies of those who pay his salary. But this, of course, is the ultimate dualism, the polarization of the people and their own institutions.[58]

He (the social worker) must then walk the tightrope between conflicting demands. If client identification is uppermost to him, he will present the case to his agency in a way most likely to garner support for a client-oriented course of action. This may require that he minimize the risk to his agency while underscoring the importance of his client's interests. He may even argue the case with more passion than he feels, if he believes that his emotional tone will positively affect his . . . administrative support. He will, in short, engage in political behavior.[59]

As Mary McCormick observed:

Risk . . . is taken in one form or another whenever a professional man or woman believes that human welfare is threatened and that his involvement will somehow alleviate or remove that threat. Commitment like this is serious, demanding, and often frustrating.[60]

One option open to the worker is to become a radical operating within the system to bring about the needed change in society. As Rein stated: "Workers can act as rebels within a bureaucracy, humanizing its established procedures and policies."[61]

Another option is for society to value highly the advocate role by attempting to institutionalize the role of the ombudsman.

The ombudsman . . . receives complaints from citizens who feel that they have been mistreated by government, . . . is an insider with full access to confidential files; . . . is chiefly concerned with those situations in which the bureaucracy exceeds its authority and fails to follow approved procedure, i.e., the problem of administrative abuse.[62]

Objection to the ombudsman role was raised, not so much on philosophical grounds, but on pragmatic issues such as the limited authority of the ombudsman. It is "not a substitute for basic reform and . . . only basic reform will achieve justice for the poor." It was also criticized because it "promises the poor a good deal more than it can deliver."[63]

Whether the social worker acts as ombudsman, enabler, expediter, or facilitator, the intended goal is to meet the needs of the client by "negotiating effectively with the organizations in which the satisfaction of their (the clients') needs may depend." The worker, serving as troubleshooter, social reformer, or innovator, is constantly reminded of his responsibility to operate within a "liberalistic, democratic, and humanitarian social philosophy and a strong sense of social obligation."[64] These responsibilities include:

1. his need for knowledge and skills in individual and group helping procedures;
2. his readiness to assume an activist type of helping role, that is, he must be direct, self-assertive, and influential in intervention in social systems;
3. his need to make a more conscious, direct, and "therapeutic" use of authority, so as to alter power structures, communication patterns and community resources;
4. his democratic use of authority which allows freedom of choice for the client;[65]
5. his obligation to inform every client "that he has God-given and inalienable rights guaranteed to him under the Constitution," that society has no right to ignore him, and that he does not live in "the best of all possible worlds";[66] and
6. his responsibility to move out of the foreground of visibility, influence, and power, into the background where he uses his skill and sensitivity to develop and train those whom he serves.[67]

With the reintroduction of advocacy, social work took on a new look during this period. A wider range of interventive methods and techniques were now at the worker's disposal. Efforts in intervention were to extend from those involving solely the client and his family or group to those which focused upon the social systems and social institutions of the client's world.

ENDNOTES FOR CHAPTER 7

1   Merlin A. Taber and Anthony J. Vattano, "Clinical and Social Orientations in Social Work: An Empirical Study," *Social Service Review*, March 1970, pp. 34-36.
2   Ibid.
3   Alfred J. Kahn, "The Societal Context of Social Work Practice," *Trends in Social Work Practice and Knowledge* (New York: National Association of Social Workers, 1977).
4   Ronald A. Feldman and Harry Specht, "The World of Social Group Works," *Social Work Practice: 1968* (New York: Columbia University Press, 1968), pp. 79, 81.
5   Alan D. Wade, "The Social Worker in the Political Process," *The Social Welfare Forum: 1966* (New York: Columbia University Press, 1966), pp. 56-57.
6   Scott Briar, "The Current Crisis in Social Casework," *Social Work Practice: 1967* (New York: Columbia University Press, 1967), p. 22.
7   Charles Garvin and Paul Glasser, "The Bases of Social Treatment," *Social Work Practice: 1970* (New York: Columbia University Press, 1970), p. 154.
8   Carol H. Meyer, "Casework Below the Poverty Line," *Social Work Practice: 1965* (New York: Columbia University Press, 1965), p. 234.
9   Ibid, pp. 234-35.
10   Ibid., p. 235.
11   Werner W. Boehm, "Toward New Models of Social Work Practice," *Social Work Practice: 1967* (New York: Columbia University Press, 1967), p. 4.
12   Wade, "Social Worker in the Political Process," p. 58.
13   Ibid.
14   Ibid., p. 60.
15   Alvin L. Schorr and Edward C. Baumehier, "Social Policy," *The Encyclopedia of Social Work*, 16th ed. (New York: National Association of Social Workers, 1971), pp. 1361-362.
16   Robert Perlman, "Social Planning and Community Organization: Approaches," *The Encyclopedia of Social Work*, 16th ed. (New York: National Association of Social Workers, 1971), p. 1338.
17   Robert Perlman and Arnold Gurin, "Perspectives on Community Organization Practice," *Social Work Practice: 1967* (New York: Columbia University Press, 1967), pp. 69-70.
18   Boehm, "Toward New Models," p. 8.
19   Richard M. Titmuss, "Social Policy and the Economic Process," *The Social Welfare Forum: 1966* (New York: Columbia University Press, 1966), p. 38; Sanford Jolender, "The Challenge to Social Welfare in

America," *The Social Welfare Forum: 1963* (New York: Columbia University Press, 1963), p. 21.

20 Harlan Cleveland, "International Implications of Social Goals," *The Social Welfare Forum: 1962* (New York: Columbia University Press, 1962), p. 57.

21 Charles I. Schottland, "Federal Planning for Health and Welfare," *The Social Welfare Forum: 1963* (New York: Columbia University Press, 1963), p. 119.

22 Bernard Coughlin, "Community Planning: A Challenge to Social Work," *Social Work*, October 1961, p. 40.

23 Helen Harris Perlman, "Social Work Method: A Review of the Past Decade," *Social Work*, October 1965, p. 173.

24 Tom Hayden, "Colonialism and Liberation as American Problems," *Politics and the Ghetto*, ed. Roland L. Warren, (New York: Atherton Press, 1969), p. 186.

25 Daniel Thursz, "Social Action," *Encyclopedia of Social Work*, 16th ed. (New York: National Association of Social Workers, 1971), p. 1189.

26 Ibid., p. 1191.

27 Arnold Gurin and Joan Levin Echlein, "Community Organizations: For Political Power or Service Delivery?," *Social Work Practice: 1968* (New York: Columbia University Press, 1968), p. 3.

28 Ibid., p. 7.

29 Melvin B. Mogulof, *Citizen Participation* (Washington, D. C.: The Urban Institute, 1970), p. 93.

30 Peter H. Rossi, "Power and Politics: A Road to Social Reform," *Social Service Review*, December 1961, p. 360.

31 Arthur Dunham, "Community Development—Whither Bound?," *Social Work Practice: 1968*, (New York: Columbia University Press, 1968), p. 61.

32 Margaret E. Berry, "NFS Launches Mississippi Project," *Round Table*, December 1966, pp. 1-4.

33 Ellen P. Manser, Jeweldean Jones, and Selma B. Ortof, "An Overview of Project ENABLE," *Social Casework*, December 1967, p. 613.

34 George Brager and Harry Specht, "Mobilizing the Poor for Social Action," *The Social Welfare Forum: 1965*, (New York: Columbia University Press, 1965), p. 197 ff.

35 Eugene S. Collender, "Business Responsibility and Individual Opportunity," *Proceedings: 19th Annual Adirondack Workshop* (New York: The National Assemble for Social Power and Development, 1968), pp. 37-38.

36 Johnnie Tellman cited by T. George Selcott in "Social Welfare Priorities: A Minority View," *The Social Welfare Forum: 1970* (New York: Columbia University Press, 1970), p. 141.

37 Sumati N. Dubey, John B. Turner, and Magdalena Miranda, "Black Unity and Self-Determination," *The Social Welfare Forum: 1969* (New York:

Columbia University Press, 1969), p. 119.

38 Savilla M. Simons, "Social Change Implications for Policy and Practice," National Conference in Social Welfare, Los Angeles, 1964. (Unpublished paper)

39 Dan Morris, "Efforts to Involve the Poor in Social Action," *Social Work Practice: 1966*, (New York: Columbia University Press, 1966), p. 164.

40 Max Siporin, "Social Treatment: A New-Old Helping Method," *Social Work*, July 1970, pp. 22-23.

41 Max Siporin, "Private Practice of Social Work," *Social Work*, April 1961, pp. 53-57.

42 Kahn, "Societal Context," p. 37.

43 Whitney M. Young, Jr., "Civil Rights and a Militant Profession," *The Social Welfare Forum: 1965* (New York: Columbia University Press, 1965), pp. 47-49.

44 Briar, "Current Crisis," p. 26.

45 Richard A. Cloward, "An Ombudsman for Whom?," *Social Work*, April 1967, p. 117.

46 The Ad Hoc Committee on Advocacy, "The Social Worker as Advocate: Champion of Social Victims," *Social Work*, April 1969, pp. 16-17.

47 Briar, "Current Crisis," p. 28.

48 George A. Brager, "Advocacy and Political Behavior," *Social Work*, April 1968, p. 6.

49 Ad Hoc Committee on Advocacy, "Social Worker as Advocate," p. 17.

50 Paul A. Kurzman and Jeffery R. Solomon, "Beyond Advocacy," *Social Work Practice: 1970* (New York: Columbia University Press, 1970), p. 67.

51 Ibid., p. 68.

52 Briar, "Current Crisis," p. 29.

53 Ad Hoc Committee on Advocacy, "Social Worker as Advocate," p. 19.

54 Briar, "Current Crisis," p. 30.

55 Ad Hoc Committee on Advocacy, "Social Worker as Advocate," p. 18.

56 Ibid., p. 21.

57 Brager, "Advocacy and Political Behavior," p. 7.

58 William Schwartz, "Private Troubles and Public Issues: One Social Work Job or Two?," *The Social Welfare Forum: 1969* (New York: Columbia University Press, 1969), p. 31.

59 Brager, "Advocacy and Political Behavior," p. 7.

60 Mary T. McCormick, "Social Advocacy: A New Dimension in Social Work," *Social Casework*, January 1970, p. 10.

61 Martin Rein, "Social Work in Search of a Radical Profession," *Social Work*, April 1970, p. 23.

62 Martin Rein and Frank Reissman, "A Strategy for Anti-poverty Community Action Programs," *Social Work*, April 1966, pp. 7-8.

63 Cloward, "An Ombudsman for Whom?," p. 118.

64 Siporin, "Private Practice," p. 54.
65 Siporin, "Social Treatment," pp. 21-23.
66 Young, "Civil Rights," p. 47.
67 Kurzman and Soloman, "Beyond Advocacy," p. 71.

CONCLUSION

As this study comes to a close, it might be observed that a history of client self-determination is really a mini-history of the totality of social work. And this should come as no surprise if we recall the pervasive nature of self-determination. It influences all of social work and in turn it is influenced by everything in social work. The study of its origin, growth, and development could not have been told or understood without reference to the political, social, and economic currents in the American scene, nor without the multiple happenings in the profession's theory and practice.

As its growth and evolution unfolded, fifty years may have occasionally seemed to be interminable; yet, the period of five decades is considerably shorter than the average life-span of a person in this country. This may suggest that the struggle of the social work profession to clarify its value system and its basic operative principles (of which client self-determination is a major one) has really just begun. Very probably, it is a never-ending labor.

In the early decades, the principle was the statement of an ideal, expressed in brief and simple terms, exhortatory and evangelistic in tone. At the end of the fifth decade, the terminology was still relatively simple, but the sermonizing ceased entirely; the brevity gave way to a fullness that resulted, in part, from a more formal and explicit exploration of social work values.

Initially, and for at least the first two decades, social work literature dealt with client self-determination almost exclusively as it applied to the casework method, chiefly because the theory of group work, community organization, and social action were comparative late-comers on the social work scene. This changed in the turbulent sixties. The literature reflected the aggressive struggle of minorities to secure their civil rights. This struggle hurried the development of community organization and social action as helping methods. The essential meaning of the battle for civil rights was, precisely, freedom. That is, self-determination achieved by changing the unjust social institutions and structures. Long gone was the social work objective of "helping people adjust to their environment." The environment was declared unjust. It denied rights and had to be changed. How much of this change was actually accomplished is difficult to say; a number of additional years are necessary for a true historical assessment. But in some social agencies and community groups, the recipients of social services won representation on policy-setting, planning, and decision-making boards. They clamored not merely for participation but for control. The latter demand achieved minimal success.

The essential components of the theory of client self-determination were recognized at the end of the third decade, as presented in Chapter 4 of this study. In the last two decades there were no basic abrogations of what preceded, but there were many refinements and developments. The 1950 formulation was tested, confirmed, and enriched by the socioeconomic developments of the time, new knowledge, the development of new methodological theories, and the rise of new problems. Each of these is briefly summarized in the following paragraphs.

The *socioeconomic events* in the fifties and sixties which most directly affected social work's commitment to client self-determination were the wars in Korea and Viet Nam, the cold war with Russia, and the domestic civil rights struggle. The issue in each of these was the safeguarding of democracy abroad and at home, and the fight for a full measure of civil rights for the minorities. These events made the national atmosphere a friendly place in which the principle of client self-determination could flourish. Legal decisions in five cases, *Topeka*, *Newburgh*, *La Fountain*, *Gideon*, and *Gault* favored human rights and self-determination.

Four sources of *new knowledge* helped to refine client self-determination. Ego psychology reinterpreted the role of the ego as an active cause, potentially very effective in personality development. The rediscovery of the importance of culture, especially in the science of cultural anthropology, enhanced social work's knowledge of man's relationship to his environment, past and present. Role theory helped to systematize the profession's knowledge of the multiple and intricate social relationships in the life of a person. The three major conferences on values, described in Chapter 6, attempted to analyze the philosophical base of social work, and in so doing inevitably confronted the intricacies of self-determination.

The *new practice models* of problem-solving and behavior modification were added after 1950 to the diagnostic and functional models. The behavior modification model was challenged as a violator of client self-determination; the early debates on this charge made interesting reading and revealed fresh nuances in the interpretation of client self-determination. The introduction of advocacy as a new role for the social worker also pinpointed a few new thoughts about client freedom.

A persistent question throughout fifty years was the relevance of self-determination to some categories of clients. In the early decades the question referred to the aged, children, clients in correctional settings, and to public assistance clients. Later the reference was to the multi-problem client, the nonvoluntary client, the retarded or mentally ill client, and the institutionalized patient. Were some types of people to be excluded from self-determination? Was it impractical in some settings with some clients? Universality was favored. The old dictum was invoked: if one person is deprived of freedom, the freedom of all is endangered.

As 1970 began, the principle of client self-determination was a relatively peaceful topic in the social work profession. It stirred no strong controversies. It was generally accepted as the second most important value and as a necessary ingredient of good professional practice. There was still no generally accepted formulation of the principle, and there was no strongly felt need for a formal definition, except in schools of social work. There were still many questions and problems of theory and practice, but they were causing little discomfort except to teachers and students.

This peacefulness most probably will not last forever. An event, a happening can shatter it: a happening such as a new political, social, or economic policy; an occurrence such as a significantly new knowledge development; or a circumstance such as the introduction of a drastically new helping method. When that happens, the dormant embers will again be fanned into a flame and another reexamination of the principle of client self-determination will be called for. It will become the story of another decade.

INDEX

Adolescents, 42
Advocacy, 15, 22, 170-75
Aged, 16, 69-70, 110
Agency function, 80, 97-98
Aronowitz, Eugene and
  Weinberg, Denise, 151
Attitudes of social workers,
  17-22, 42-44
Authority, 34-37, 58, 60, 63, 67,
  78-80, 97, 112-13, 152-53

Bandura, Albert, 152-53
Behavior modification, 150-53
Bernstein, Saul, 54, 131
Biestek, Felex P., 73-83

Bisno, Herbert, 94
Boehm, Werner W., 163
Bowers, Swithun, 93
Briar, Scott, 160, 172
Brisley, Mary S., 15
Bruck, Max, 152
Bruno, Frank J., 10, 11, 24

Cannon, Mary A., 12
Capacity of client, 13, 33-34, 62,
  76-77
Casework, 54-58, 104, 181
Chakerian, Charles G., 129-30
Character disorders, 103-04
Children, 67-69, 110-11

185